"I do not understand why God's world co[illegible]
nor why shared suffering often brings th[illegible]
such inspiring goodness. *Unbroken Faith* names both the darkness and light in ways that will comfort, challenge, and re-awaken the ache of hope."

—**John Ortberg**, senior pastor of Menlo Church, Menlo Park, CA, and author of *I'd Like You More If You Were More Like Me*

"With raw authenticity and sensitivity, Diane helps me understand the unspoken cries of a special-needs parent, and offers guidance on how to love, support—and most importantly—do life together."

—**Kathi Lipp**, speaker and best-selling author of *The Husband Project*, *Overwhelmed*, and *Clutter Free*

"*Unbroken Faith* exceeds my expectations. What Diane has discovered through this journey of disability is a valuable lesson for us all."

—**Kara Ferris**, Executive Director, iamviable.org

"With authenticity and deep understanding, Diane writes from her heart to ours. The special-needs journey from broken hearts to unbroken faith, from vague diagnosis to victorious living, from demolition to renovation, from failed hopes of the ideal to the reality of the real. . . . she covers it all and brings us the hope we seek!"

—**Dr. Joe and Cindi Ferrini**, authors of *Unexpected Journey: When Special Needs Change Our Course*

"Diane Dokko Kim wrote the book she wished had been available to her family when she and her husband first learned their son has an autism spectrum disorder. She effectively uses Scripture to help families understand more about God and how His character and purposes are revealed through their experience with disability."

—**Stephen Grcevich M.D.**, president and founder of Key Ministry, Chagrin Falls, OH

"*Unbroken Faith* is a *must* read for *every* parent of a child with special needs. This is my new number one resource to give to every newly diagnosed family with special needs in our ministry!"

—**Stephen "Doc" Hunsley, M.D.**, pastor of Grace Church, Overland Park, KS, SOAR Special-Needs Ministry Director, and special-needs parent

"Diane is a gifted communicator who has an amazing passion to see families find true rest and fellowship in the Church through Jesus. God will use *Unbroken Faith* to empower, equip, and comfort families who are hurting, and teach the larger church body how to be the hands and feet of Jesus in real and meaningful ways."

—**Rebecca Barnett**, Board Certified Behavior Analyst (BCBA), Special-Needs Ministry Coordinator, Menlo Church, Menlo Park, CA

"In *Unbroken Faith*, you will find a candid yet compassionate guide who will lead you from feeling overwhelmed, discouraged, and inadequate to living with renewed belief, courage, and hope."

—**Cheri Gregory**, co-author of *Overwhelmed*, co-host of *Grit 'n' Grace*, and co-leader of Sensitive and Strong

"Diane's book is a much needed tool for any parent in the trenches of raising a child with disabilities. Bravo, Diane, and thank you."

—**Jami Amerine**, author of *Stolen Jesus: An Unconventional Search for the Real Savior*

"*Unbroken Faith* meets a profound need. Scripturally sound, it is a fantastic tool to help facilitate validation, emotional healing, and most importantly, spiritual growth. I am thrilled and proud to recommend this resource to churches who want to help special-needs parents grow in a relationship with Jesus Christ."

—**Amy Fenton Lee**, author of *Leading a Special-Needs Ministry: A Practical Guide to Including Children and Loving Families* and blogger at theinclusivechurch.com

"In *Unbroken Faith*, Diane Dokko Kim is unflinchingly honest about the spiritual battles she fought as the mother of a child with special needs. She traces the path through the Word that erased her doubts and led her to solid ground again. Best of all, she fills *Unbroken Faith* with promises from Scripture to encourage and equip other parents coming to terms with God's plans for their children. If you are one such parent, you need to read this book."

—**Jolene Philo**, author of *Different Dream Parenting: A Practical Guide to Raising a Child with Special Needs*, and special-needs parent

"Diane Dokko Kim shares with great transparency her journey of faith as the parent of a son with autism. Beautifully written and theologically sound, *Unbroken Faith* offers powerful encouragement and spiritual sustenance by helping parents understand that they are not alone."

—**Lorna Bradley D.Min.**, author of *Special-Needs Parenting: From Coping to Thriving*

"I wish I had this book years ago. If you find yourself in the unique, scary, exhausting, unknown world of special-needs parenting, I encourage you to run—not walk—to get *Unbroken Faith*."

—**Shelly L. Welsh**, M.A., LMFT, former disability ministry director, and special-needs parent

"When faced with the unimaginable—like a special-needs diagnosis for your child—the world suddenly feels lonely and your faith fragile. What you need most in this undone place is a tender soul who gets it and a guide to help you navigate every hard step of the way. This book is that guide and Diane Dokko Kim that soul. You are not alone, friend."

—**Michele Cushatt**, author of *Undone: A Story of Making Peace with an Unexpected Life*

"Reading *Unbroken Faith* is rather like sitting down for coffee with a wise and wonderful friend. Diane fully captures the experience of raising a child with special needs—the grief, trauma, exhaustion, and the unparalleled joy as well."

—**Katie Wetherbee, M.A.**, learning specialist at Notre Dame College and author of *Every Child Welcome: A Ministry Handbook for Including Kids with Special Needs*

"Diane writes with a vulnerable, almost painful, transparency regarding the journey of a special-needs parent. Her raw emotions give permission to other parents to grieve, argue, question, and doubt. Diane does not merely share her angst. Instead, she reveals how her angst points her to God in new way. It reminds her of complete dependence upon him and of just how true all of the promises of the Bible are. Be blessed and encouraged and filled with hope as you read this book over and over again."

—**Mike Dobes**, Joni and Friends Church Relations Manager

"Parents who are navigating the world of disability with their children desperately need this book. Diane asks the hard questions many are afraid to ask and answers with faith-filled honesty and humor."

—**Debbie Lillo**, co-author of *Doing Life Together: Building Community for Families Affected by Disability*, Joni and Friends Church Relations Manager

"*Unbroken Faith* offers hope to parents as they cling to Jesus through the daily challenges of raising a child with special needs, and an authentic glimpse into the heart of a mom whose faith and love for her child is unwavering. I would recommend this book, not only to families affected by disabilities, but to those who care about them as well, or to anyone who needs a reminder that Jesus understands our deepest hurts and can do incredible things in them."

—**Jeanette Hanscome**, author of *Suddenly Single Mom: 52 Messages of Hope, Grace, and Promise*

"As a professional, having dedicated a better part of eighteen years to the special-needs population, this book is *exactly* what I have been looking for. As a mother of a child with special needs, I truly appreciate Diane's honesty and her ability to explain, to the core, what it's like to be the forever caretaker of another human being. This book is beautifully done."

—**Dr. Julie H. Lee**, Licensed Marriage Family Therapist (LMFT),
founding intervention specialist at the Intellectual Virtues Academy,
lecturer at California State University, Fullerton,
and special-needs mother

"*Unbroken Faith* is wisdom not just for the parent of the special-needs child, but for all of us who have faced brokenness in ourselves or our loved ones. I give *Unbroken Faith* my highest endorsement. I thank Jesus for the refining and transformational work He is doing in Diane Dokko Kim, and for those who are brave enough to pick up this book in search of deeper understanding."

—**Cynthia Zierhut**, Ph.D. Clinical Psychologist,
former Research Psychologist at UC Davis MIND Institute,
Champions Director at Capital Christian Center,
owner of Early Days Autism Center

UNBROKEN *faith*

UNBROKEN *faith*

spiritual recovery
FOR THE
special-needs parent

DIANE DOKKO KIM

Published by Worthy Books, an imprint of Worthy Publishing Group, a division of Worthy Media, Inc., One Franklin Park, 6100 Tower Circle, Suite 210, Franklin, TN 37067.
WORTHY is a registered trademark of Worthy Media, Inc.

Helping people experience the heart of God

eBook available wherever digital books are sold.

Library of Congress Control Number: 2017960857

Published in association with the literary agency of Kirkland Media Management, LLC doing business at P.O. Box 1539, Liberty, Texas 77575.

ISBN: 978-1-68397-134-4

Cover Design: Jeff Jansen | AestheticSoup.net
Interior Layout: Bart Dawson

Printed in the United States of America
18 19 20 21 22 23 LBM 10 9 8 7 6 5 4 3 2 1

To my enduring husband, Eddie
To our boys, Jeremy and Justin
And to my ever-supportive parents
There is no this without your sacrifice.
Thank you.

CONTENTS

FOREWORD

By Joni Eareckson Tada

BEFORE YOU BEGIN . . .

As our Joni and Friends' teams serve special-needs parents around the world, we've found a common thread: parents feel isolated and exhausted. When the shocking diagnosis comes—during pregnancy, at birth, in childhood, or after an illness or accident—these parents are hit with sorrow and deep disappointment. Their hopes for the future are shattered and their dreams are completely dismantled. Even the most stalwart Christians experience a crisis of faith. My friend Diane Dokko Kim is one.

Diane intimately understands the heart of a special-needs parent. When she and her husband, Eddie, were given a diagnosis of autism for their young son Jeremy, their world turned upside down. Although they had returned from the mission field and were deeply rooted in their church, their faith was rocked to the core. They questioned God's kindness and struggled with the shame and guilt imposed by others. Sadly, they mistakenly thought their faith left no room for anger or doubt. It only made things worse.

I first got to know Diane and Eddie at Mission Springs Family Retreat, shortly after Ken and I wrote *Joni and Ken: An Untold Love*

Story. In it, we share the heartbreaking struggles that come with disability in a marriage. Diane resonated with that transparency. The Kims yearned to understand how my marriage to Ken had withstood so many assaults. Diane wanted what she saw in our book—she longed to encourage others with what she was learning as a mother and wife.

And she has done just that. Diane is a gifted speaker and writer—her blog is widely followed by parents and church leaders across the country. Her gift? She's *authentic.* Although she deeply loves her children, Diane shares a raw response to the pain she's experienced. Her reflections are mixed with humor and sobriety, and she helps readers laugh at their own circumstances. Diane has looked God in the eye and confessed her inability at times to trust Him: "God, are You *really* 'close to the brokenhearted,' as You tell me in Psalm 34:18?"

When parents hear Diane speak, or when they read her articles and blog, they find someone who gets it, someone who understands. Often for the first time since the diagnosis of their child's disability, they can say, "Finally! I've found another parent who truly resonates with my struggles!"

Unbroken Faith is offered as medicine for a hurting heart. Diane pulls back the curtain on some of the toughest faith questions asked by parents of children with special needs. She points you to the Word of God in hopes that you will experience heaven-sent comfort and compassion. She will help you grasp how God understands your pain and how He suffers with you. In this extraordinary book, Diane reassures you of God's goodness, reminding you that it's okay to grieve . . . weep . . . doubt . . . and to ask the hardest of questions.

Diane's book is an excellent resource for support groups or Bible studies. It is a valuable tool for any church leader, friend, or family member who wants to better nurture the hearts of special-needs parents. Whether you are a pastor or a family counselor, *Unbroken*

Faith will enlighten you to the hidden challenges every parent of a disabled child faces.

Bless her heart, Diane recently told me that she wished a book like *Unbroken Faith* would have been available during her darkest years—it would have been a great help, she said. It's why my friend has written *Unbroken Faith.* Her insights on the following pages are her gift to you, and she earnestly prays it'll be a balm to your soul. Be ready to have your heart stirred . . . as you read the precious book you hold in your hands, be ready to be transformed!

Joni Eareckson Tada
Joni and Friends International

The world breaks everyone and afterward
some are strong at the broken places.

Ernest Hemingway, *A Farewell to Arms*

Introduction

"JUST A PIECE OF PAPER"

For the word of God is alive and active.
Sharper than any double-edged sword, it penetrates
even to dividing soul and spirit, joints and marrow;
it judges the thoughts and attitudes of the heart.
Hebrews 4:12 NIV84

It was just a piece of paper, weighing less than an ounce. But it was the heaviest burden I would ever hold. Some papers cut deeper than others: divorce papers, a Do Not Resuscitate form, or even a pink slip. Are they "just a piece of paper"? Hardly. From the moment of issue, each triggers cataclysmic changes for the recipient and ripples out from the epicenter to impact the lives of everyone surrounding.

On August 20, 2004, a four-by-six-inch piece of paper leveled my world, when a pediatric neurologist scribbled onto a prescription pad and slid it across his desk:

> Patient meets diagnostic criterion 299.00 of the DSMIV. Moderate to severe autism. Severely disabled. Mentally retarded. Cognitively impaired. Non-verbal. Aggressive intervention of 40 weekly hours of applied behavioral analysis, speech therapy, occupational therapy, plus ancillary supports strongly advised. Prognosis unknown.

After months of speculation, evaluations, and dread, our firstborn was diagnosed with autism. Like BC and AD divide world history, autism would cleave my narrative into two distinct eras: Before and After.

Spiritual Code Blue

As I grieved the death of my idealized child, well-meaning church friends attempted to console with encouraging words and Bible verses.

> *"God won't give you anything you can't handle."*
> *"Special-needs children are a blessing!"*
> *"Trust God. He is good!"*

Just stop. Please. In the face of *Severely disabled. Mentally retarded. Prognosis unknown,* how is disability a blessing? How is God still good? Our son was cognitively disabled; and I was now spiritually crippled. That single piece of paper severed all existing connections between my head and heart. Any preexisting conditions, convictions, and even feelings went numb as disillusionment and spiritual death hovered near. My faith was flatlining. We *both* required urgent and intensive intervention.

"God Understands"?

Spiritual surgery is not without pain. Pat Sunday-school answers are as helpful as a Band-Aid plastered hastily over a stab wound. Superficial solutions don't stick. Shallow treatment doesn't mend torn tissue or flush out the emotional pus festering deep within. Sometimes you have to cut deep to really deal with what's going on inside.

"For we do not have a high priest who is unable to sympathize with our weaknesses, but we have one who has been tempted in every way, just as we are—yet was without sin. Let us then approach the throne of grace with confidence, so that we may receive mercy and find grace to help us in our time of need" (Hebrews 4:15–16 NIV84).

But what does the Bible have to do with the modern-day, gritty realities of raising a child with a disability? How is this antique, archaic book relevant? What does God know about special needs parenting? *His* Child was perfect, wasn't He? An impenetrable, omnipotent Being didn't have to contend with chronic fatigue, isolation, or a lack of resources and support. After all, He has all the power of the universe at His disposal. What does God really understand about this?

Consider this: In Genesis, He knows the joyful anticipation of beloved children. He prepared lavishly for their arrival, too, just like every eager parent. He also understands the heartache when those children don't turn out as expected, despite having done everything right to guarantee they do. And His heart was filled with pain.

In Isaiah, He's the Father of a wounded Son who was bullied, misunderstood, rejected, and scorned. He shares my outrage, feral protectiveness, and demand for justice. He advocates for us. Oh, how He fights for us! He knows when we are unable to fend for ourselves. His strength is perfect in our moments of abject weakness. He vindicates to make our righteousness shine like the noonday sun.

At Gethsemane, He felt completely alone, carrying a burden no one could understand. He experienced utter disappointment when trusted people weren't there for Him at His time of need. He cried out prayers in blood, sweat, and tears . . . that were met with silence. He, too, pleaded for deliverance but received the answer no. He even uttered the same words I've cried out in times of darkness and despair: "My God, why have you forsaken me?" (Mark 15:34).

At the cross of Calvary, for all His power and authority—being in very nature God—He demonstrated submission to "not my will, but thine" (Luke 22:42 KJV). He proved "my grace is sufficient for thee" (2 Corinthians 12:9 KJV). Ultimately, He demonstrated His power over death and despair. He proved that what the enemy intended for evil, God can redeem for good (Genesis 45:5). He proved that He is a redeeming God, the only kind of God He knows how to be.

Faith Rehabilitated

What I thought guaranteed certain death became the primary vehicle for proving God's goodness and the relevance of His Word. The Word of God suddenly became absolutely relevant to the struggles and doubts of a special-needs parent. Knowing that the God of the universe understands how I feel, and hurts as I hurt, somehow makes a difference. He *gets* it. He gets *me*.

Astonishing.

The Word of God *is* living and active. Sharper than any double-edged sword, it penetrates even to dividing soul and spirit, joints and marrow; it judges the thoughts and attitudes of the heart. For those willing to submit to its scalpel, it wields supernatural skill to sear through the scar tissue of cynicism, cauterize a hemorrhaging heart, and flush out the toxic bile of bitterness. It has power to bind up and heal that which is broken.

The Bible is no ordinary, historical piece of literature. It isn't just a thick compilation of paper. It is the very Words of Life, able to defibrillate a dying faith and infuse it with new resilience and vitality. If a single piece of paper could wreck my life in an instant, then over one thousand divinely inspired pages wields infinite power and authority to resurrect, redeem, and repurpose.

The Word of God has transformed my life. I pray it transforms yours.

CHAPTER 1

"Do Not Be Afraid!"

GOOD NEWS, GREAT FEAR

And there were shepherds living out in the fields nearby, keeping watch over their flocks at night. And angel of the Lord appeared to them, and the glory of the Lord shone around them, and they were terrified. But the angel said to them, "Do not be afraid. I bring you good news that will cause great joy for all the people."
Luke 2:8–10

A phone call in the middle of the night, or from our child's school in the middle of the day: both flood a parent's heart with instant dread. Before a single word is spoken, our hearts brace for impact our ears have yet to receive. For years after our son's diagnosis and enrollment in special-education classes, his teacher prefaced every midday call home with, "Hi. Don't worry. Everything's fine. We just need ________."

Sometimes it was a missing permission slip. Other times it was to notify us of a mild bump or bruise he'd sustained on the playground. And of course, there were the "difficult" days, when an uptick in behaviors or ill health necessitated a call home.

As a veteran special-education professional experienced in interfacing with anxious parents, she anticipated the pre-elevated stress of a special-needs parent. She preemptively sought to assuage it. No matter how severe or mundane the reason, every call came preceded by "Don't worry . . ." because she knew we'd worry.

Of course we'd worry. Special-needs parents are people forever changed by unexpected news.

Good News, Great Fear

"Fear not" is one of the most oft repeated exhortations in the Bible. Within the first two chapters of Luke, an angel of the Lord disseminated good news to three parties whose fates were intertwined: Zechariah, a priest tending to his temple duties when startled and gripped with fear (1:11–13); a betrothed young maiden, Mary, greatly troubled, wondering what kind of greeting this might be (1:28–31); and shepherds tending to their flock, when accosted by heavenly hosts in the dead of night (2:9–10).

Each had been faithfully tending to their God-given responsibilities when interrupted. They could not have prepared for the news they were about to receive. The bewildering message and the shocking manner of delivery were frightful enough. To a geriatric Zechariah: "Your wife Elizabeth will bear you a son, and you are to call him John" (Luke 1:13). To a young virgin: "You will conceive and give birth to a son, and you are to call him Jesus" (Luke 1:31). To the shepherds who hastened to Bethlehem: "You will find a baby wrapped in cloths and lying in a manger" (Luke 2:12).

"Good news of great joy" was met by great fear. Zechariah wondered in his heart, *How can I be sure of this?* and Mary in hers, *How will this be?* What normal person wouldn't be terrified? It would have been abnormal *not* to be afraid. "Good news that will cause great joy for all the people" (Luke 2:10) was stunning and exhilarating at best, alarming and dreadful at worst. Yet each responded to the confounding favor of God with a faith that defied their incredulity.

How Is This Good News?

> *Your child has autism. He'll need at least forty hours of intensive therapy a week. He may not learn to speak, function, or live independently. He'll likely not go to college, marry, or have his own family. You'll have to abort your plans and rearrange your lives to care for him full time. His prognosis? Unknown. You'll have to just wait and see.*

Our child's lifelong prospects—all the unspoken possibilities every new parent assumes as a birthright—had suddenly been snuffed out. Our toddler could barely walk when his future suddenly ran out on him. How could this be? How would his life turn out? How would *our* lives turn out? All-encompassing fear crowded out space for anything else. Rather than soothe, well-intentioned exhortations of "Don't worry. Don't be afraid. Just trust God!" only aggravated an already troubled heart.

In the world's economy, a diagnosis of disability is hardly "good news." To a parent, it's the worst news in the world. The sudden upheaval of lifelong plans are legitimately terrifying. In that moment, it would have been utterly mindless and insensitive for anyone to dare tell us, "Do not be afraid!" Any normal parent would be stricken with grief and dread.

Providence anticipates our shock, fear, and dread. He knows we are terrified and stricken. He has compassion for our aversion to things too marvelous for us to comprehend (Job 5:9). He is wise to greet us with eternal words of assurance, "Do not be afraid." The same God who comforted terrified shepherds, a startled priest, and an innocent young maiden comforts us in our terror and bewilderment of today. The eternal Spirit of God comes upon us to assure, "Do not be afraid! Your prayer has been heard. You have found favor with God." Though we may not understand our circumstances now, though our hearts are filled with fear, His promises bring good news of great joy that will benefit all people: our children, our extended families, and our communities.

When stricken at a child's diagnosis, take heart. We stand in good company. Heavenly hosts once heralded the most terrifying and wondrous news to a handful of frightened sheepherders in the dark. Despite their terror and astonishment, the thrill of hope drove them to Bethlehem, where they were amazed to find all the things "just as they had been told" (Luke 2:20).

God has the audacity and authority to prelude our journey with "Do not be afraid!" because He already knows how our story will unfold. A sovereign God already knows the future that awaits our child and the inconceivable blessings that wait for us. He who can birth life from barrenness, inject peace into chaos, and spring life from death can transform the most shocking news and redeem it for our good (Romans 8:28). For nothing is impossible with God. He has done it before, and He will do it again. Despite the terror that threatens to keep us paralyzed in the dark, let us respond with a supernatural faith that propels us toward His light. Fear not. Go and see. We, too, will be amazed to find things just as we have been told.

UNBREAKABLE PROMISES

- "So do not fear, for I am with you; do not be dismayed, for I am your God. I will strengthen you and help you; I will uphold you with my righteous right hand" (Isaiah 41:10).
- "The LORD is my light and my salvation—whom shall I fear? The LORD is the stronghold of my life—of whom shall I be afraid?" (Psalm 27:1).
- "You will keep in perfect peace those whose minds are steadfast, because they trust in you" (Isaiah 26:3).
- "'For I am the LORD your God who takes hold of your right hand and says to you, Do not fear; I will help you. Do not be afraid . . . for I myself will help you,' declares the LORD, your Redeemer, the Holy One of Israel" (Isaiah 41:13–14).
- "God is our refuge and strength, an ever-present help in trouble" (Psalm 46:1).
- "Peace I leave with you; my peace I give you. I do not give to you as the world gives. Do not let your hearts be troubled and do not be afraid" (John 14:27).
- "When I am afraid, I put my trust in you" (Psalm 56:3).
- "Be strong and courageous. Do not be afraid or terrified because of them, for the LORD your God goes with you; he will never leave you nor forsake you" (Deuteronomy 31:6).

Prayer

God of comfort, we confess our fear and dread about our child's diagnosis. You already knew how this would terrify us. You go ahead of us with understanding, patience, and compassion. You also know how our child's life and our family's story will unfold.

Though we cannot imagine how this could possibly be "good news," we claim Your promises, goodness, and faithfulness in advance, no matter how we may feel. Fill us with Your presence. Enable us to defy our natural fears with supernatural faith in You.

Questions

1. What was your initial reaction—thoughts or feelings—to the news of your child's diagnosis? How did you respond?
2. What are your biggest fears or worries for your child's future and that of your family?
3. What is your "Bethlehem"? What are the next steps you can take to support your child and family while also working on your faith?

CHAPTER 2

"What More Could I Have Done?"

WHEN CHILDREN DON'T TURN OUT AS EXPECTED

What more could have been done
for my vineyard than I have done for it?
When I looked for good grapes,
why did it yield only bad?
Isaiah 5:4–5

In the final months leading up to the birth of our first child, my husband and I delighted in a common rite of passage for expectant parents: the baby registry. Armed with a digital scanner, we scampered about the baby section of Target. We tagged items, paying no regard to price or quantity. Giddy with possibility, we ventured into aisles with items we wouldn't need for years: dictionaries, science kits, bicycles, and musical instruments. Anything and everything felt like ours for the taking.

Back at home, we washed organic cotton onesies on the delicate setting and gingerly tucked away baby shower gifts. The freezer was stocked, checklists checked and double-checked, suitcases packed and repacked for good measure. The only thing pending was the baby's arrival. Life was beautiful, promising, and good. So very good.

Then, an unexpected diagnosis. The sudden abort of dreams. The emotional whiplash from a jubilant "It's a boy!" to a hushed "I'm so sorry . . ." was swift and staggering. We expected parenting to be challenging. Sleepless nights, we signed up for. But no book or website could have prepared us for this. Disability barged into our home uninvited, with no forewarning or instructions.

What more could we have done? We had done everything we could to prepare perfection for our child. Why did we get disability instead?

It Was Very Good

In the opening chapters of Genesis, the first Parent in history prepared lavishly for the arrival of His firstborn. He outfitted the universe with unparalleled artistry and enthusiasm. The God who made the heavens and the earth and everything in it, He spared no expense. He saw all that He had made, and it was good. But nothing compared to the glory of His ultimate creation: His children. Only then was the creation *very* good (Genesis 1:31).

Then, a mere two chapters into the infancy of humanity, sin snuck in. Doubt, distrust, and disorder broke out like a disease run rampant. The chaotic descent from joyous birth to shock and dismay was steep, devolving into a downward spiral of wounding and being wounded. These perfect children . . . God became grieved in His Spirit that He had made them at all, and His heart was filled with pain (Genesis 6:6). He prepared perfection.

The glory of creation was now irreparably marred. Defective. Ebullient hope and promise had sunk on its maiden voyage. How could a breach happen so soon? A loving Father had ensconced His beloved in the middle of paradise. He provided His utmost to guarantee their fruitfulness, blessing, and joy. Why did they turn? Why did they yield disappointment and sorrow instead? What more could He have done?

God Understands

What more could I have done for my child? After all I've done to secure their health and happiness, why did we get this? When I planned for perfection, why did it yield heartbreak instead?

Our heavenly Father understands our outrage and grief. He, too, intended perfection for us, His children: plans to prosper and not to harm us, plans to give us hope and a future (Jeremiah 29:11). The perfect Parent did everything possible to ensure His children's joy and fulfillment. It was not for lack of intention, wisdom, or preparation. There was nothing more He could have done.

We grieve the loss of what could have been. Our Father understands and grieves with us. Yet for every parent who mourns, the ultimate Abba is also at work to exchange beauty for ashes, the oil of joy for mourning (Isaiah 61:3). God understands our heartache, but He does far more than that. He redeems it.

Despite His profound loss and heartache, the heavenly Father immediately launches a disaster recovery plan. From the Garden of Eden, to the cross at Calvary, and over every crushing disappointment today, our God is still a Redeemer. It's the only kind of God He knows how to be.

Immeasurably More

After the Fall, no parent could ensure their child would be born blemish-free. When the enemy injected doubt into paradise, dissension and discord ensued. Our physical, spiritual, and emotional hardwiring—once perfect—followed suit.

Take comfort in God's original design for His children. Despite the wiles of a broken and capricious planet, His character remains the same. He is still the God of good, good, and very good.

The Lord is the same yesterday, today, and forever (Hebrews 13:8). He remains committed to our sanctification, wholeness, and perfection. We may be in the genesis stages of our journey as a special-needs family, but He is already at work. God will prevail over what we could not prevent. Just as He knew the Genesis story would resolve in Revelation and beyond, He also already knows how our glory story will unfold. It will be immeasurably more than we can imagine.

UNBREAKABLE PROMISES

- "Blessed are those who mourn, for they will be comforted" (Matthew 5:4).
- "My soul is weary with sorrow; strengthen me according to your word" (Psalm 119:28).
- "Is there no balm in Gilead? Is there no physician there? Why then is there no healing for the wound of my people?" (Jeremiah 8:22).
- "For you created my inmost being; you knit me together in my mother's womb. I praise you because I am fearfully and wonderfully made; your works are wonderful, I know that full well. My frame was not hidden from you when I was made in

the secret place, when I was woven together in the depths of the earth. Your eyes saw my unformed body; all the days ordained for me were written in your book before one of them came to be" (Psalm 139:13–16).

Prayer

Lord, You prepared Your utmost for Your children. You had high and lofty expectations for us. But we didn't turn out according to Your original plans. I take comfort in knowing You understand and share in our heartbreak. You grieve with me and over me. Help us to trust in Your original plans for very good. *You are still a* very good *God.*

Questions

1. In what significant or unique ways did you prepare for your child's arrival?
2. How have you had to adjust your expectations and plans for your child and family?
3. How is God shaping your character or challenging your ideals about parenting?

CHAPTER 3

"This Is Not the Way It's Supposed to Be!"

WRECKED: FROM HALLOWED TO HOLLOWED

When it was almost time for the Jewish Passover, Jesus went up to Jerusalem. In the temple courts he found people selling cattle, sheep and doves, and others sitting at tables exchanging money. So he made a whip out of cords, and drove all from the temple courts, both sheep and cattle; he scattered the coins of the moneychangers and overturned their tables. To those who sold doves he said, "Get these out of here! Stop turning my Father's house into a market!" His disciples remembered that it is written: "Zeal for your house will consume me." The Jews then responded to him, "What sign can you show us to prove your authority to do all this?" Jesus answered them, "Destroy this temple, and I will raise it again in three days." They replied, "It has taken forty-six years to build this temple, and you are going to raise it in three days?" But the temple he had spoken of was his body. After he was raised from the dead, his disciples recalled what he had said. Then they believed the scripture and the words that Jesus had spoken.

John 2:13–22

Perhaps the early years of childhood flew by in a blissful blur, just as they should. Until subtle hints began to emerge: A missed developmental milestone, then another. The sinking sense of a pattern developing while our child did not. A series of dissonant mental notes that kept growing louder, only no one else seemed to hear.

"All kids do that. My child was late with that too."

"You're being paranoid. Stop overreacting. I'm sure he's fine."

"He'll grow out of it. All children develop differently."

All we knew for certain was an unnerving sense of: *Something's just not right. This is not the way it's supposed to be.* Either the baby books and websites were wrong, or something else was.

Or perhaps an ultrasound detected signs of genetic anomaly, the physical evidence confirming itself at birth. Long-held silent prayers and closeted dread went unanswered, until now. Regardless of how gradual or sudden the onset, a child's diagnosis slams into a family with brutal, blunt force.

Precious, dewy-eyed perfection is ravaged. The unblemished, inviolable child we thought we had is no longer. With our child's potential plundered, righteous indignation consumes us. All that could have been—all that should have been—is now impossibly out of reach. Our lives violently overturned, our hearts wail in protest, *This is not the way it's supposed to be!*

Zeal for God's House

In John chapter 2, Jesus entered God's holy temple to find it degenerated into a marketplace. Irreverence and contempt trafficked through sacred space, leaving filthy tread marks in its wake. Consecration had devolved into desecration. Hallowed reverence gave way to hollow religion. Commerce and convenience encroached on a covenant, and the heavens shuddered at the travesty. *This is not the way it's supposed to be!*

Perfect communion had been spoiled, an irreconcilable difference wedged between a holy God and His unrighteous people. The guilty stain soiled our pristine connection and we lapsed beyond repair. Beloved children slinked back to hide in shadowy spaces of fear, guilt, and blame—intolerable conditions for a loving Father.

God burns with anger to see His sacred temple ravaged. Whatever pollutes the purity of our worship appalls Him. In His zeal for God's house, Jesus will overturn anything that diseases our wholeness, our holiness. For we are the temple of the living God, our bodies the temples of the Holy Spirit, who dwells in our midst (1 Corinthians 3:16). We were meant to be holy, blameless, and pure children of God without fault (Philippians 2:15). Our souls were made to strive for perfection as our heavenly Father is perfect (Matthew 5:48).

That's the way it was supposed to be.

Rebuilt, Restored, Redeemed

> "Destroy this temple, and I will raise it again in three days."
> —John 2:19

Impossible. Or so it would seem to human eyes. "But the temple he had spoken of was his body" (John 2:21, emphasis added). Subject to the divine authority of God, no destruction is final. Even death could not keep Him in the grave (Acts 2:24). He who has power to resurrect from the dead has absolute authority to hallow what's been hollowed.

Our heartache is but a shadow of our Father's grief over us all. Revulsion is perfectly appropriate when purity is defiled. This is not the way it's supposed to be. The loss of perfection was never God's intention. We mourn the unspeakable loss of potential, the forfeiture of the full measure of all that could have been. Though we all fell tragically short of the glory of God, He Himself will bridge the irreconcilable differences. Our Savior is in the very business of salvaging the unsalvageable. God will redeem and repurpose. But His restoration plan may not look like ours.

> Imagine yourself as a living house. God comes in to rebuild that house. At first, perhaps, you can understand what He is doing. He is getting the drains right and stopping the leaks in the roof and so on: you knew that those jobs needed doing and so you are not surprised. But presently He starts knocking the house about in a way that hurts abominably and does not seem to make sense. What on earth is He up to? The explanation is that He is building quite a different house from the one you thought of—throwing out a new wing here, putting on an extra floor there, running up towers, making courtyards. You thought you were going to be made into a decent little cottage: but He is building a palace. He intends to come and live in it Himself.
>
> —C. S. Lewis[1]

Renovation and rebuilding always start with demolition. The Master Builder is not interested in mere cosmetic upgrades. When the Lord rebuilds, it may not look as we expect. No eye has seen, no ear has heard, and no mind has ever conceived the glorious things God has prepared for those who love Him (1 Corinthians 2:9). His dwelling place will be among the people, and He will dwell with them. They will be His people, and God Himself will be with them and be their God (Ezekiel 37:27). He will wipe every tear from their eyes. There will be no more death or mourning or crying or pain, for the old order of things will pass away. Behold, He is making all things new (Revelation 21:3–5).

Only let us believe the scripture and the words that Jesus has spoken. In a little while, He will fill His house with His glory (Haggai 2:6–7). Jesus restores hallowed, hollowed spaces: past, present, and future. Demolition and rebuilding are labor-intensive, grueling processes. Through it, He *will* restore all things to the way they were meant to be.

UNBREAKABLE PROMISES

- "Passion for your house has consumed me, and the insults of those who insult you have fallen on me" (Psalm 69:9 NLT).
- "You turned my wailing into dancing; you removed my sackcloth and clothed me with joy" (Psalm 30:11).
- "You realize, don't you, that you are the temple of God, and God himself is present in you? No one will get by with vandalizing God's temple, you can be sure of that. God's temple is sacred—and you, remember, *are* the temple" (1 Corinthians 3:16 MSG).
- "'Though the mountains be shaken and the hills be removed, yet my unfailing love for you will not be shaken nor my covenant of peace be removed,' says the LORD, who has compassion on you" (Isaiah 54:10).
- "Anyone who shows respect for the LORD has a strong tower. It will be a safe place for their children" (Proverbs 14:26 NIRV).

Prayer

Lord, this is not how it's supposed to be. This is not how I imagined our child's life, my life, or my family's future. I am comforted that You understand. You are even more outraged and angry than I am. You intended infinitely more for us. Help me believe the scripture and the words You have spoken: You rebuild, restore, and redeem sacred space, whether in this lifetime or the next. This includes my child, and it includes me.

Questions

1. What were some initial indications of "Something's just not right" in your child's development?
2. What "should have been" do you grieve the loss of? What expectations, hopes, or dreams do you fear can no longer be?
3. What "new thing" might God be building for you? What work of rebuilding and redemption is God working in you?

CHAPTER 4

"Where Do I Go with My Pain?"

PERMISSION TO GRIEVE

*When I kept silent, my bones wasted away
through my groaning all day long. For day and night
your hand was heavy on me; my strength
was sapped as in the heat of summer.*

Psalm 32:3–4

"*He's such an easy baby! He never seems to cry or cling!*"

As the saying goes, there can be too much of a good thing. Our baby was *too* easy. He rarely fussed or demanded. Our darling preschooler saw everyone but connected to no one; heard everything but responded to nothing. He would snatch away toys from other children, oblivious to their protests. Nor did he complain when other children took away his. For us, the typical toddler soundtrack of "Mommy, mommy, mommy!" never came.

How we wished it would. We had no idea what the signs of

autism were, only a nagging sense of something vaguely amiss. Finally, summoning the courage to book an appointment, we found ourselves seated reluctantly at the pediatrician's office. The doctor kindly received my laundry list of concerns. Her bemused expression hinted I was yet another paranoid, first-time mother who believed everything she googled on the Internet.

Meanwhile, Jeremy wandered about the office, entirely uninterested in a conversation that only dissected his deficiencies. He found his way to a metal examination table and crawled underneath. I was in the middle of explaining how he never communicated his needs, not even when he was hungry or in pain. Just then, as if on cue, Jeremy stood up abruptly and smacked his head against the underside of the table. Hard.

The pediatrician and I swiveled around, anticipating an outburst of wails. But he just stood there silently, blinking back tears. Slowly, he reached his hand up to touch the place of impact. He looked bewildered. How dare the sky crash down, so rudely without warning.

Not once did he look up. He never saw me or made a sound. No crying or seeking comfort. Mother and medical personnel stood by in rapt attention less than five feet away, on high alert. But it was as if he was in the room alone.

After a pregnant pause, the pediatrician turned slowly toward me. Her expression softened, visibly shifting gears from clinician to counselor. She formulated her next words with great care, *"I, uh. I think we may have something here . . ."*

Silent Suffering, Silent Wasting Away

"When I kept silent, my bones wasted away through my groaning all day long."

Psalm 32 refers to the burden of guilt from unconfessed

sin. But guilt and grief steal and undermine our spirits in similar ways. Acutely aware of how our expectations have fallen short, our grief lies ever before us. The fullness of joy—all that should have been—has been exiled, leaving an unbearable void that aches. Oppressed by a weight we cannot dislodge, we groan over pain we're unable to name. Our souls are pierced. And we bleed until we're drained of hope. Spiritual gangrene festers until all signs of life are but wasted away.

Yet we feel obligated to suppress our anger. We paste on our "good Christian" mask for our church friends and force out Bible verses through clenched teeth: all in a valiant attempt to "fake it till we make it." As if an all-knowing God might be offended to find out how we really feel. He isn't fooled. He saw how our child's diagnosis pounced like a terrorist attack. He was there the moment a single piece of paper, a diagnostic report, ambushed to bludgeon our minds and devastate our hearts.

Our heavenly Father knows we are stunned, bewildered, and reeling from shock at a world that crashed on us without warning. He has compassion for our spiritual paralysis. As we grieve the hit our children have sustained, so does our Father grieve over ours. Our heavenly Father aches to comfort us in our sufferings. But when we refuse to acknowledge our wounds, our spirits cannot properly heal. Instead, we may try to camouflage the hurt or grow a superficial layer of coping over it. We attempt to shake it off and stumble along. But our refusal to be honest about our feelings only hinders us from accessing the very source of comfort, soothing, and healing.

Leaning In, Not Away

A child's natural instinct at pain is to cry. An indignant howl of protest or even a yelp would have been appropriate. But my child's odd, unnerving reaction indicated something was amiss. He was trying to process what had just struck him. But he never sought my help. As his mother, anything that assailed him was an affront to me too. Parents hurt when their children hurt. But it pained me even more that he didn't seek my comfort. Watching him suffer, seeing him unable to seek my help, that grieved me the most. I ached to soothe and reassure him. But he did not permit me the opportunity.

Subsequent tests confirmed that Jeremy's inability to seek out help in times of distress was indicative of a social and relational disorder, just like our refusal to instinctively run to our heavenly Father is indicative of our spiritual and relational disorder. Our Father knows we are wounded. He grieves when we know not where to go with our pain. Our hurts are made worse when we suffer in silence. The God who desires truth in our innermost being (Psalm 51:6 NASB) grieves to see us remain isolated and paralyzed in our suffering.

Where do we go with our pain? When we keep silent, when we suppress our tears, our bones waste away needlessly. Let not your spirit wither away. Whether we run to Him or keep silent, whether we acknowledge our outrage at the sky's falling or not, our heavenly Father knows. He hurts over and with us, on our behalf.

Let us permit our Father access, allow Him to coax our stunned tears into release. Our Father longs to gather His children together, like a hen gathers her chicks under her wing (Matthew 23:37). Let us not suffer alone, isolated in our spiritual autism, disconnected from our heavenly Father. He is the source of all hope and healing, both in body and mind, soul and spirit. Let us approach our Father's throne of grace with confidence, so that we may receive mercy and find grace to help us in our time of need (Hebrews 4:16).

UNBREAKABLE PROMISES

- "In him and through faith in him we may approach God with freedom and confidence" (Ephesians 3:12).
- "Let us then approach God's throne of grace with confidence, so that we may receive mercy and find grace to help us in our time of need" (Hebrews 4:16).
- "In the same way, the Spirit helps us in our weakness. We do not know what we ought to pray for, but the Spirit himself intercedes for us through wordless groans. And he who searches our hearts knows the mind of the Spirit, because the Spirit intercedes for God's people in accordance with the will of God." (Romans 8:26–27 NIV).

Prayer

Lord, something in me keeps me from running to You with my pain. You desire nothing more than to comfort my wounded heart. Thank You for the permission and grace to be honest about my hurt. I welcome it. I need it. I cannot heal until I allow myself to be real.

Questions

1. In what ways are you processing your pain, anger, or grief? Where or to whom have you turned? Are there healthier or more productive alternatives to foster emotional healing?
2. Have you given yourself permission to grieve? Have you told God honestly how you feel, or do you feel unable to turn to Him?

3. Take a moment to list all your areas of grief and perceived loss. Speak authentically and honestly with God, knowing He understands and shares your pain.

CHAPTER 5

Angry "with" God

LEANING IN, NOT AWAY

In your anger, do not sin; when you are on your beds,
search your hearts and be silent.
Offer right sacrifices and trust in the Lord.
Psalm 4:4–5 NIV84

Christmas Eve 2005, our extended family drove six hours to rendezvous at an amusement park renowned for its manicured gardens and family-friendly rides. Everyone looked forward to festive merriment and a buffet no one had to cook or clean up.

Hordes of other families must have thought the same. The park was packed. Holiday lights cast flickering shadows into the night. Shrubbery sculpted into the shape of circus animals pumped out cheery Christmas carols through hidden speakers: ambient to us, but shrill to the sensitive ears of our son. Dancing animatronics puppets charmed every youngster but ours, who only found them terrifying.

Eventually, the clashing odors of french fries, perfume, and diesel fuel proved to be too much. Fifty feet past the entrance gate, Jeremy began to gag. His body revolted, thrashing him against the concrete. His father wrestled to contain him while relatives stood by, helpless. Horrified onlookers gawked and seemed to judge us with their eyes. *What a terrible child! What terrible parents!*

After fifteen minutes of sweaty struggle, my husband abandoned any notion of merriment and dragged our writhing child back to the minivan. Wedged between the crawl space of padded seats and tinted windows, Jeremy unleashed the full magnitude of his fury at his father. Jeremy's dad, too, was free to unfurl *his* rage and frustration in the presence of his Father. Both heaved and howled against a hostile world, safely ensconced in upholstered grace.

Brokenness in a Broken World

Like many on the autism spectrum, Jeremy's sensory processing is disordered. To him, the world is a volatile and inhospitable place. Whenever his universe explodes, we retreat to a quiet place to shield him from harm and judgment. At times, we're forced to drag him against his will. He may inadvertently kick, strike, and fight against us. But we know not to take it personally. His outbursts are an involuntary response to being attacked. We forgive, for he knows not what he does. Given his hapless hardwiring, his instincts are pardonable. But causing injury to himself or others is not. In his woundedness, we do not permit him to wound.

"In your anger, do not sin . . ." (Ephesians 4:26).

The Bible presumes our anger at a world that refuses to function as it should. No one is spared its jagged edges—not even the Almighty Himself. His wrath burned at Israel's unfaithfulness throughout the Old Testament. Jesus overturned tables at seeing the temple of the Lord dishonored. And at Calvary, the earth split, the skies went dark, and the heavens rumbled at the cosmic injustice of the Son of God, crucified. "Nobody gets through a broken world unbroken," aptly said author and theologian Dr. Ed Stetzer.

Anger in the Wrong Direction

Anger itself is not a sin. But what we do with that anger, if we process it destructively, can be. Joni Eareckson Tada wrote in "Anger: Aim It in the Right Direction":

> All of our emotions are corrupted by sin. We need to bring our anger and hurt—and all the rest of our emotions—into the transforming presence of God. If we fail to submit our anger to God, that anger leads us away from God—that's "unrighteousness anger." It allows strong feelings of displeasure against God and His choices or actions in our life to foment and fester. An unrighteous anger breeds mistrust of God, and eventually, loathes dependence on God. . . . The biblical way to handle anger is to be transparent before the Lord, while at the same time not blaspheme or badmouth Him, turn your back on him, or sow seeds of discord about Him. Rather than say things you'll only regret later, learn how to complain in a godly way! Don't move away from God . . . move towards Him. Don't turn your back on God . . . face Him. It's the biblical and constructive way to resolve your anger.[2]

Righteous anger can drive us toward God. Like the anguish that fills the books of Psalms and Lamentations, we, too, can write our own book of psalms. We must choose to lean into Him, not away. It is the difference between being angry *at* God and being angry *with* God, for He grieves our suffering too.

Angry "with" God

> The irony of questioning God is that it honors Him; it turns our hearts away from ungodly despair toward a passionate desire to comprehend Him (Dr. Dan Allender).[3]

Our questions and anger over our child's disability can drive us closer into the presence of God, if we let it. Henri Nouwen, in his foreword to *May I Hate God?* wrote, "[T]he anger and hatred which separate us from God can become the doorway to greater intimacy with Him . . . It is clear that only by expressing our anger and hatred directly to God will we come to know the fullness of both His love and His freedom."[4]

Perhaps we expect our parenting journey to be blissful, like a stroll in the park at Christmas. Wholly unprepared for the ambush that awaits us, our plans get hijacked. A sudden diagnosis strikes and throws us to the ground. Life betrays our most precious, unspoken expectations, leaving us senseless and screaming at the skies.

Disability is not what we planned for. We are permitted righteous anger. Anything that undercuts or undermines all God intended angers Him too. He shares our indignation and demand for justice. This was not the way it is supposed to be.

"Just as a father has compassion on his children, so the LORD has compassion on those who fear Him. For He Himself knows our frame; He is mindful that we are but dust" (Psalm 103:13–14 NASB).

When grief depletes us of reason and we lash out blindly, our Father enfolds us in safety. When we push and pull away in bitterness and blame, He endures our outbursts with longsuffering. He suffers and grieves our losses with us. He is strong enough to contain our rage, compassionate enough to quell it, and magnanimous enough to overlook it. He is big enough to handle our meltdowns without taking offense and does not treat us as our sins deserve. He forgives us, for He knows we know not what we do.

Ever the sensitive and attuned parent, the Lord knows when we are distressed beyond our capacity and bids us retreat with Him to a quiet place (Mark 6:30–32). He longs that we lean in toward Him, not away, to find compassion and grace in our time of need.

A diagnosis—or any devastating news—can be a dangerous opportunity. Biblical scholar Leonard W. Pine concludes, "Far from being a sin, proper remonstration with God is the activity of a healthy faith relationship with Him."[5] God invites us to engage with Him, to be angry *with* Him. After all, where could we flee from His Spirit? Where could we flee from His presence? (Psalm 139:7) Held tightly in the boundaries of grace, we need never fear falling too far. Jesus knows how it feels to be overwhelmed to the point of death (Mark 14:34). We find no greater solidarity, solace, or soothing than the safety of His embrace.

UNBREAKABLE PROMISES

- "If only my anguish could be weighed and all my misery be placed on the scales! It would surely outweigh the sand of the seas—no wonder my words have been impetuous" (Job 6:2–3).
- "I remember my affliction and my wandering, the bitterness and the gall. I well remember them, and my soul is downcast within me. Yet this I call to mind and therefore I have hope: Because of the LORD's great love we are not consumed, for his compassions

never fail. They are new every morning; great is your faithfulness" (Lamentations 3:19–23).

- "Who shall separate us from the love of Christ? Shall trouble or distress or persecution or famine or nakedness or danger or sword? . . . For I am convinced that neither death nor life, neither angels nor demons, neither the present nor the future, nor any powers, neither height nor depth, nor anything else in all creation, will be able to separate us from the love of God that is in Christ Jesus our Lord" (Romans 8:35, 38–39).

Prayer

Abba Father, I'm sick with fury and overwhelmed by a world that has crushed my hope. I want to punch and pull away, but You draw me in for my own protection. Thank You for creating a safe space for me to be angry with You.

Questions

1. What circumstances or settings trigger extreme reactions for you?
2. Are you angry *at* God or *with* Him? How would they look different for you? In being angry with God, what might you think, feel, say, or do differently?
3. Who or what can help you safely work out your feelings of grief and being overwhelmed? Identify safe people or places where you can retreat.

CHAPTER 6

"Don't You Care, God?"

WRITING OUR OWN PSALMS

How long, LORD? Will you forget me forever?
How long will you hide your face from me?
How long must I wrestle with my thoughts and day after day
have sorrow in my heart? How long will my enemy
triumph over me? Look on me and answer, LORD my God.
Give light to my eyes, or I will sleep in death, and my enemy will say,
"I have overcome him," and my foes will rejoice when I fall.
But I trust in your unfailing love; my heart rejoices in your salvation.
I will sing the LORD'S praise, for he has been good to me.
Psalm 13

A rogue wave called autism had struck, leaving me sputtering with shock and indignity. In its wake, I was swept along into a career change I never signed up for: full-time caregiver, case manager, disability advocate, and traffic controller. Now my days were spent floundering amidst the waves of therapeutic professionals who cycled in and out of our home, specialists I'd never heard of before with a dizzying array of acronyms: LSW, ABA, OT, SLP, BCBA. Daily, for forty hours a week, as soon as one wave rolled out, another rolled in.

Dipping into the reserves of a faith bottomed out, I sagely accepted my new calling: Help the Poor Child. A forced perma-smile betrayed clenched teeth that gritted out my new mantra, "I'm trusting God. I'm trusting God. I'm trusting God . . ." But inside, I was wrecked. Our son was cognitively disabled; I was now spiritually crippled. Both of us needed urgent and intensive intervention. But therapists only came for him.

Late into the night, after all dishes, children, and toys had been tucked away, after another Google search for a cure came up empty, the house would finally fall quiet. With my façade of professionalism wiped away with the day's makeup, only then, all the suppressed tears and dammed-up anguish were finally permitted to give way.

Are You there, God? Don't You care? How could You let this happen? How long must we suffer like this?

Night after night, I howled at the heavens, daring it to smite me with lightning. None came. Spent, weary, and feeling foolish from screaming at skies that never responded, I began funneling all my bottled-up rage into a private journal. Where else could I go with my ravings? Housebound, broke, and too ashamed to seek counseling, a password-protected document became my rock in the ground, a secure place to dump all the sick and sour that bubbled up from a diseased heart.

What did God have to do with this? Where was He? How was the Bible relevant anymore, if at all? I fought with His words, and He graciously contended with mine. These outpourings become sacred space for a nightly, spectator-less wrestling match between my God and me.

Five eternal years and two battered keyboards later, I had pounded out my own book of psalms.

Heaving Heavenward

The book of Psalms is the longest in the Bible. Out of 150 chapters, half are lamentations. Anguished and authentic, terrible and wondrous, the outpouring of raw and conflicted emotions mirrors our own: chaos and confusion, outrage and earnestness, fear and failure, yearning and despair.

> My God, my God, why have you forsaken me?
> Why are you so far from saving me,
> so far from my cries of anguish?
> My God, I cry out by day, but you do not answer,
> by night, but I find no rest.
> —Psalm 22:1–2

> Will the Lord reject forever?
> Will he never show his favor again?
> Has his unfailing love vanished forever?
> Has his promise failed for all time?
> Has God forgotten to be merciful?
> Has he in anger withheld his compassion?
> —Psalm 77:7–9

When the Bible dedicates a significant portion of its real estate to acknowledge human pain and suffering, who are we not to? Rather than being hushed, silenced, or admonished to behave more "holy," the psalmists were permitted to gush unfiltered expressions of heartache directly before the throne of God. Raw and unfiltered, their earnest outpourings benefit future generations who wonder if God hears or sees them in their suffering. What are humans that He should be so mindful of our feelings? How extraordinary that God honors and validates our struggles!

Writing Our Own Book of Psalms

The psalmists pave the way for us special-needs parents. They give us permission to be vulnerable and honest before the Lord too. When our emotions flood out all reason, our hearts can align with the cries of the psalmists who lend words when we lack the ability to articulate them for ourselves:

> How long, Lord? How long do we have to suffer like this?
> I cry out to You, night after night. I ask for deliverance, for help, for hope, for answers. But I get nothing.
>
> Do You care? Are You even there? Why won't You answer our prayers and do something? Why won't You fix this? If You're really God, how easy that would be for You! Can You even hear me, or am I just screaming into the air?
>
> Why can't I have a normal child like everyone else? Why me? Why us?
> Why must my child suffer? Why must we suffer?
> Haven't I been faithful? Didn't we do everything we were supposed to? Why do we get this, when everyone else has it so easy? It's not fair.

> No one understands what I'm going through. I'm alone. I can't do this. I'm working as hard as I can, but nothing is ever enough. Every morning I wake up, I'm even further behind. No one knows my pain, not even my spouse, my closest friends, or family. No one gets this.
>
> Oh, and the pity! I can't stand their pity!
>
> I am broken. My heart is broken. My body is broken. My family is broken. My faith is broken. How can I do this? You say You are a good and loving God. How could that be, when we're in such pain? I need Your promises to be true. If You hear me, I need You to be realer and nearer than ever.
>
> You say You have the words of life. Where else can I go? To whom else can I turn to?
>
> Please hear us. See us. Give me hope. Give us strength and grace for tomorrow because I'm already depleted by today. This is too big for me. Please be a God who is big and powerful enough to rule over all this, because I am not.

When we're unable to pray, the Psalms can speak on our behalf to express the incoherent groanings of our spirit (Romans 8:26–27).

Our true feelings—confusion, fury, outrage—are no surprise to an omniscient God. We have permission to be real before a merciful Father. He receives and honors the cries of our hearts, and exercises the spiritual largesse to handle the failings of our human frailty. He knows that we are but dust. God alone is big enough to receive us with mercy and grace in our time of need.

As we bring our brokenness before the Lord, He can sift through our ravings and blot out our transgressions. He can create in us a clean heart and renew a steadfast spirit within (Psalm 51:10). To whom else could we turn? Where else could we go?

Weeping and worship need not be mutually exclusive (2 Samuel 12:16–20). We can grieve yet believe: process as we protest. Like David, author of nearly half of the Psalms, we, too, can be women and men after God's heart. We cry out because we seek answers. Rather than a spiritual death, questions are signs of life, however faint.

How long, O Lord? How long must we endure? Until His divine purposes come to pass in our lives. Until we can conclude along with others who cried out before the Lord and lived to tell about it:

> In my distress I called upon the LORD,
> And cried to my God for help;
> He heard my voice out of His temple,
> And my cry for help before Him came into His ears.
>
> He sent from on high, He took me;
> He drew me out of many waters.
> He delivered me from my strong enemy,
> And from those who hated me, for they were too mighty
> for me.
> They confronted me in the day of my calamity,
> But the LORD was my stay.
> He brought me forth also into a broad place;
> He rescued me, because He delighted in me.
> —Psalm 18:6, 16–19 NASB

UNBREAKABLE PROMISES

- "People of Zion, who live in Jerusalem, you will weep no more. How gracious he will be when you cry for help! As soon as he hears, he will answer you" (Isaiah 30:19).
- "Have mercy on me, LORD, for I am in distress. Tears blur my eyes. My body and soul are withering away. I am dying from grief; my years are shortened by sadness. Sin has drained my strength; I am wasting away from within" (Psalm 31:9–10 NLT).
- "When my anxious thoughts multiply within me, Your consolations delight my soul" (Psalm 94:19 NASB).
- "I am worn out from my groaning. All night long I flood my bed with weeping and drench my couch with tears" (Psalm 6:6).

Prayer

Lord, thank You for the great cloud of witnesses who have gone before me in pouring out their hearts in honesty and brokenness before You. These psalmists demonstrate that I can weep and worship at the same time, knowing You hear me and receive me.

Questions

1. Where do you go with your anger? Have you directed your feelings up? Or have you been leaking sideways? Where or to whom might your grief be unfairly spilling?
2. Which of the psalms resonates most with you? Which verse might you claim as your own?
3. Write out your own book of psalms—real, raw, and unpolished. What will you heave heavenward before the Lord?

CHAPTER 7

"Broken" Child, Broken Parent

OUR PERSONAL PENIEL

That night Jacob got up and took his two wives, his two female servants and his eleven sons and crossed the ford of the Jabbok. After he had sent them across the stream, he sent over all his possessions. So Jacob was left alone, and a man wrestled with him till daybreak. When the man saw that he could not overpower him, he touched the socket of Jacob's hip so that his hip was wrenched as he wrestled with the man. Then the man said, "Let me go, for it is daybreak." But Jacob replied, "I will not let you go unless you bless me."

Genesis 32:22–26

In 2004 our family returned from a year abroad on missions. My husband and I had taken our six-month-old infant to serve in a third-world country few had ever heard of. "It's a country next to Afghanistan" would often elicit wide eyes and impressed nods. "Ohhhhh . . ." Deep down, I considered it a pretty impressive step of faith. I was pleased others agreed. The winds of spiritual victory fueled us to serve the Lord with fresh fervor. Committing ourselves to full-time ministry, we eagerly anticipated God's confirmation and favor. Surely He had even greater blessings in store.

Then our child was diagnosed with autism.

All ebullient testimony evaporated in a nanosecond. Whatever credentials I had banked up were now gone, the balance sheet empty. The former missionary mentally crumpled up her spiritual resume and chucked it away in disgust. Now, I was nothing but furious. Everything I'd worked for, a service history and reputation that took decades to build, now felt irrelevant and remote. Outraged and indignant at being stripped bare, I demanded of the Lord, *"I will not let You go unless you bless me. Restore my stuff. Restore my child!"*

Jacob, Entitled to Retitled

Jacob was quite literally a self-made man. He stole his brother's birthright to become a man he was never entitled to be. His life was spent manipulating and being manipulated, hustling and being hustled. Sometimes victims have a way of victimizing others: hurt people hurt people. Then, the day of reckoning came. For years Jacob had successfully evaded responsibility for his shady character. The trappings of wealth and success managed to camouflage a lack of integrity.

Eventually, he had nowhere left to hide: a backlog of guilt and transgressions finally caught up with him. In great fear and distress, this lifelong grifter braced for his comeuppance. Remarkably, he was met with mercy and compassion instead. Overpowered and overcome by the Lord, he came away changed: broken. His former name of "deceiver" no longer fit. The supplanting nature of a lifelong supplanter had been supplanted. His character and outlook were irrevocably changed, and a new calling and identity were born. In spite of his failings, God had a greater vision for Jacob than any ambition he could have connived on his own.

Redemption and Restoration

Like Jacob, God's response to my tantrum was to remind me of who I was: a deceiver who lived for appearances. My true identity and impulses had been exposed. I'd been caught accumulating reputation credits as a "Super Christian," a church leader, even as a former missionary. Such duplicitous motives stank far more than the rank of all Jacob's livestock. Now that all such trappings were sent adrift, my faith was shipwrecked. Stripped and stranded, I was left alone to wrestle with who I truly was. Defrocked of all spiritual accoutrements and ornamentation, who was God in my life? What did I really seek Him for?

Yet while I was a sinner, He loved me. While I cursed my intolerable circumstances and raised my fists to the skies, the Lord exercised forbearance and compassion. Our heavenly Father is magnanimous enough to endure the petulant tantrums of His children. He looks beyond our faults to see our needs. It took several years of wrestling. My stubbornness was not easily overpowered. But my bitterness and spiritual self-entitlement were ultimately wrenched by the grace of God. But rather than getting my *stuff* restored, my *soul* was. Spiritual ambition dislodged, I could then be granted a new identity and purpose: to know and pursue the Lord. Not just His stuff.

Staking Our Personal Peniel

Special-needs parenting can be our personal Peniel, where we come face-to-face with God yet are spared. Disability—or any devastating news—presents an opportunity to walk through refining fire, to burn away the dross of demands, disillusionment, and doubts. Are we willing to wrestle through our faith crisis, however long it takes? God has a glorious new inheritance and entitlement for His children. He invites us to surrender our hustling, to pursue Him wholly for who He is, irrespective of His benefits. Those willing to be wrenched at the core emerge with a purified and more precious faith.

A life of obedience does not guarantee exemption from limping or struggle. More than a decade later, my child still has autism. I still eagerly await the day we shall all be fully restored. In the meantime, the blessings have come through "the glad surrender."[6] I used to think my son's disability—his "brokenness"—was intolerable. Now, I find myself glorying in my own. May I forever limp in humility, submission, and surrender before my God. For when I am weak He is strong.

UNBREAKABLE PROMISES

- "Therefore humble yourselves under the mighty hand of God, that He may exalt you at the proper time, casting all your anxiety on Him, because He cares for you" (1 Peter 5:6–7 NASB).
- "Blows that wound cleanse away evil; strokes make clean the innermost parts" (Proverbs 20:30 ESV).
- "You have searched me, LORD, and you know me. You know when I sit and when I rise; you perceive my thoughts from afar. You discern my going out and my lying down; you are familiar with all my ways. Before a word is on my tongue you, LORD, know it completely" (Psalm 139:1–4).

Prayer

Lord, my child's disability has wrecked me. I thought my child was "broken." But I'm the broken one, spiritually and emotionally. My child's disability may be physical and/or cognitive, but I have a hidden, spiritual disability. Sin hinders me from becoming all You intended. Help me wrestle with my doubts until I am conquered by Your grace and surrendered to Your greater purpose for our lives. Please help my unbelief. Help me dare to believe that You are working something inconceivably greater in us, for us, and through us.

Questions

1. In what ways are you broken? Over which wrenched expectations do you wrestle with God? Which blessings are you demanding to be restored?
2. What is God working to wrest out of you, to create space for new blessings he wants to pour into you? What greater work might He be trying to accomplish through your struggle?
3. How is your faith, character, identity, or purpose being challenged or transformed through your child? What blessings or insights have you gleaned?

CHAPTER 8

"Did You Lead Us Out Here to Die?"

TRAPPED BY THE IMPOSSIBLE

As Pharaoh approached, the Israelites looked up, and there were the Egyptians, marching after them. They were terrified and cried out to the LORD. They said to Moses, "Was it because there were no graves in Egypt that you brought us to the desert to die? What have you done to us by bringing us out of Egypt? Didn't we say to you in Egypt, 'Leave us alone; let us serve the Egyptians'? It would have been better for us to serve the Egyptians than to die in the desert!" Moses answered the people, "Do not be afraid. Stand firm and you will see the deliverance the LORD will bring you today. The Egyptians you see today you will never see again. The LORD will fight for you; you need only to be still."

Exodus 14:10–14

My husband and I became Christians in our early twenties and immersed ourselves in bivocational ministry. Committed to radical discipleship, we professed Christ and exhorted others to know the same God. "Taste and see that the LORD is good. Blessed is the one who takes refuge in him" (Psalm 34:8), we proclaimed. Convicted and confident of God's calling, we left home, career, and comforts to serve on missions. Our return home was heralded by a procession of ardent testimonies of God's goodness. Then, months after stepping off the plane, we hit a wall. We got slammed with autism.

What was that all about? We prayed. *Was it because there were not enough agnostics and cynics in the world that You gave us this reason to doubt? Why did You have us give all these testimonies about You, only to make us double-back on our words? It would have been better if we never followed You at all! This is what we get? This was our reward for committing to Christ?*

With so many public professions made, we'd come too far to turn back. I felt gypped, as if we'd been set up to fail in spectacular fashion. I wanted to quit: quit ministry, quit church, and quit God. *How could You do this to us? After all we've gone through to serve and follow You?* But where could we go? There was no returning our child. We couldn't opt out of autism. To renege on our recent proclamations would have been humiliating. Walled in by impossibility on every side, we could not go back; we could not bypass. We could only go through.

Led to It and through It

Boxed in between armies and sea, the Israelites' terror was understandable. So was their chagrin. They had just experienced God's miraculous deliverance and freedom from slavery. As they exited Egypt in jubilant procession, their victory march into the promised land seemed imminent. Then they hit a wall.

Unbeknownst to the Israelites, the quickest route to Mount Sinai would have deposited them squarely into the launching point of the Egyptian military. Traveling through fortified enemy territory, the children of Abraham would have had to fight their way out. An omniscient God knew this fledgling nation would not survive such a bloodletting. Out of His wisdom and compassion, He set them on an alternate course through the least impeded path: the Red Sea. There, they found themselves strategically trapped, walled in on every side with no escape route. Providence had channeled them onto a track they had no choice but to follow.

God doesn't always remove the obstacle or impossibly. Sometimes He leads His people to forge headlong into it. What appeared to the Israelites as "leading them out here to die" was providence and mercy. Not only was the Lord redirecting the Israelites out of harm's way, He was ushering them—and their detractors—into front-row seats to witness the most spectacular display of supernatural power.

You Need Only Be Still

Like the Israelites, we may feel utterly trapped. In our angst, we may regret our commitment to the Lord, or even entertain thoughts of returning to spiritual Egypt. But there is no backing out or away from our child's disability.

Hope will not disappoint, "because the love of God has been poured out within our hearts through the Holy Spirit who was given to us" (Romans 5:5 NASB).

We have no choice but to forge straightaway into the daunting impossibility of special-needs parenting. We may be longtime believers, even a spiritual leader like Moses. Or we may be a recent follower or doubter, barely keeping pace with the procession of God's people. Regardless of our spiritual tenure, we must stay the course, even if only to trudge along the outer perimeter of fellow sojourners.

When we are overwhelmed and fearful of the waves of

impossibility that swell before us, we can be still and know that He is God. He hems us in, behind and before. He strategically places us within His assembly, to optimally experience His providence and protection. God is the same yesterday, today, and forever. His faithfulness in the past cannot help but splash into the present and spill over into our future.

Whatever diagnosis or disaster threatens to overtake us, know that He did not lead us out here to die. *"Do not be afraid. Stand firm and you will see the deliverance the Lord will bring you. The Lord will fight for you; you need only to be still."* The same voice that sliced through seas and walked over water whispers to us today, "Whether you turn to the right or to the left, your ears will hear a voice behind you, saying, 'This is the way; walk in it' (Isaiah 30:21). The journey will yield spectacular displays of God's power and provision far beyond anything we left behind in our "normal" life in Egypt.

UNBREAKABLE PROMISES

- "When you pass through the waters, I will be with you; and through the rivers, they shall not overwhelm you; when you walk through fire you shall not be burned, and the flame shall not consume you" (Isaiah 43:2 ESV).
- "You are from God, little children, and have overcome them; because greater is He who is in you than he who is in the world" (1 John 4:4 NASB).
- "You hem me in behind and before, and you lay your hand upon me. Such knowledge is too wonderful for me, too lofty for me to attain. Where can I go from your Spirit? Where can I flee from your presence?" (Psalm 139:5–7).
- "The angel of the LORD camps around those who fear God, and he saves them" (Psalm 34:7 NCV).

Prayer

Lord, You are the God who reigns over the impossible. Nothing is too difficult for You. Though I stand overwhelmed, help me to trust that You will equip and empower me for the calling You have given me to parent my child. Help me to see how You are positioning us for greater displays of Your power.

Questions

1. Recall a past "Red Sea" experience—a personal storm or time of barrenness—where you felt trapped. What did you find on the other side? What past providences reassure you of God's future faithfulness?
2. What pressing impossibilities do you face today? What do you feel trapped by? What merciful redirection might providence be leading you to?
3. How is God working on your character, motivations, and faith through "impossible" situations to prepare you for greater things to come?

CHAPTER 9

"If Only You Had Done Something!"

COULDN'T VS. WOULDN'T

"Lord," Martha said to Jesus, "if you had been here,
my brother would not have died. But I know that even now
God will give you whatever you ask." Jesus said to her,
"Your brother will rise again." Martha answered,
"I know he will rise again in the resurrection at the last day."
Jesus said to her, "I am the resurrection and the life.
The one who believes in me will live, even though they die;
and whoever lives by believing in me will never die.
Do you believe this?" "Yes, Lord," she replied,
"I believe that you are the Messiah,
the Son of God, who is to come into the world."

John 11:21–27

"If only God had stopped this!"

"If only God had intervened!"

"If only God would heal!"

Months of denial, followed by dreaded evaluations with doctors, then referrals to specialists; desperate prayers, fasting, and asking others to pray and fast with us—and we still got autism.

Years of experimental medications "not yet approved by the FDA"; trekking to foreign countries in search of holistic treatment; countless hours and dollars spent on therapies—and we still have autism.

How could God let this happen to our child? If only He had done something! If He could have intervened to stop the disability, why didn't He? If He can heal in an instant, why doesn't He?

"But . . . Lord!"

—(But) "when he heard that Lazarus was sick, he stayed where he was two more days."

—(But) "if only You had been here, my brother would not have died!"

—"But Lord, by this time there is a bad odor, for he has been there four days."

—"But some of them said, 'Could not he who opened the eyes of the blind man have kept this man from dying?'"

"But Lord! If only . . ." is the cry of every believer in the face of disappointment and heartbreak. If only God had done as we asked! We concede that God has power and authority to do as He wills. Yet we protest when He exercises that power in a way that doesn't align with our wishes. We believe God is able to answer our prayers. Our problem is accepting when He doesn't. We can't call Him "Lord!" and not do what He says (Luke 6:46); We can't call him "Lord!" and reject what He does.

Martha struggled to reconcile what she believed about Jesus with what she wanted from Him. Her freedom to protest was born out of an inviolable relationship with her Lord. Room to complain or challenge is a privilege granted only to those with whom there is implicit trust. Lazarus's death was not the first time Martha accused Jesus of failing to care. Earlier, she even dared to rebuke Him (Luke 10:40). Like children who reserve their worst tantrums for their parents, Martha's outburst was a sign of intimacy and closeness.

Martha could run to her Lord with her worst, assured He would receive her with His best. *"But I know that even now God will give you whatever you ask."* "But . . ." was immediately bookended with ". . . *Lord*." Despite her anguish, she affirmed Jesus's authority. *"Yes, Lord. I believe that you are the Messiah, the Son of God, who is to come into the world."*

To her credit, she acknowledged that the created have no right to tell the Creator what to create, or how to manage that which He created. An all-knowing God retains the right to override our short-term demands with His eternal purposes. Despite her disappointment, Martha acknowledged the God of the universe was not beholden to her preferences, and she submitted to His sovereignty.

"If only He had been there. If only He had done something." Raising a dead man to life is more dramatic than healing a sick one. An omnipotent God had power to intercede, prevent, or heal Lazarus, even from a distance (John 4:49–52). But He chose not to. What may have appeared as callous disregard was God's perfect plan unfolding. Jesus knew Lazarus's sickness would not end in death. His delay held divine purpose: so that the glory of God could be revealed.

Jesus had power to intervene. But in that moment, He was addressing Martha's faith. He paused for her, for them, and for us. God has always been concerned with our spiritual, not just physical, healing. As Martha acknowledged, our bodies will rise again in the resurrection, when our earthly bodies will be free of all burden, disease, and disability. In the meantime, Jesus initiates the restoration of our faith, today.

"Even If He Does Not . . ."

Deep down, we blame God for allowing our children to be disabled. "Why didn't He do something to stop this? If He has the power to intervene and fix this, why won't He?" Like Martha, we may believe in God's power and authority. We give mental assent that an omnipotent God is able to heal. Yet we find it difficult to accept when He doesn't. When God doesn't do as we ask, He has His reasons. The Lord is not slow in keeping His promises. Should He tarry, it is because He holds a higher purpose we may not be privy to. It is for His maximum glory, resulting in our utmost wonder. It's natural to feel indignant when God appears to refuse our wishes. But make no mistake. His failure to comply is not a lapse in His goodness, trustworthiness, or love.

This sickness, disability, or spiritual depression will not end in death. No, it is for God's glory so that God's Son may be glorified through it (John 11:4). Jesus assures that if we believe, we will see the glory of God (John 11:40).

We should only expect the unexpected of a mysterious God. He may heal. He may not. We may have to wait through agonizing days, years, or even our earthly lifetime. Ultimately, we know that our bodies will be made perfect at the resurrection. In the meanwhile, like Martha, we can profess God's authority, even as we protest it. "But Lord, even now, I believe!" (John 11:21-22).

UNBREAKABLE PROMISES

- "What I always feared has happened to me. What I dreaded has come true. I have no peace, no quietness. I have no rest; only trouble comes" (Job 3:25–26 NLT).
- "These trials will show that your faith is genuine. It is being tested as fire tests and purifies gold—though your faith is far more precious than mere gold. So when your faith remains strong through many trials, it will bring you much praise and glory and honor on the day when Jesus Christ is revealed to the whole world. You love him even though you have never seen him. Though you do not see him now, you trust him; and you rejoice with a glorious, inexpressible joy. The reward for trusting him will be the salvation of your souls" (1 Peter 1:7–9 NLT).
- "The sufferings we have now are nothing compared to the great glory that will be shown to us. Everything God made is waiting with excitement for God to show his children's glory completely. Everything God made was changed to become useless, not by its own wish but because God wanted it and because all along there was this hope: that everything God made would be set free from ruin to have the freedom and glory that belong to God's children" (Romans 8:18–21 NCV).

Prayer

Lord, I confess my frustration. I believe You are able to heal, but I'm conflicted that You don't. If only I could respond in faith, trust, and surrender! You are God, and I am not. Lord, have Your way with me, my child, and our family.

Questions

1. What are your "if onlys" where you wish God would intervene? When your desires don't appear to align with God's plan, what else might He be seeking to accomplish?
2. Which is more difficult to accept, that God can heal or that He won't?
3. What higher purposes, unexpected blessings, or gifts are being revealed in your faith, character, family, and/or community through God's "noncompliance"?

CHAPTER 10

"Why Won't You Fix This? Don't You Care?"

GOOD GIFTS

"Ask and it will be given to you; seek and you will find;
knock and the door will be opened to you.
For everyone who asks receives; the one who seeks finds;
and to the one who knocks, the door will be opened.
Which of you, if your son asks for bread, will give him a stone?
Or if he asks for a fish, will give him a snake? If you, then,
though you are evil, know how to give good gifts
to your children, how much more will your Father in heaven
give good gifts to those who ask him!"
Matthew 7:7–11

In the weeks following the diagnosis, a new regime overtook our home. A zealous adherence to "early intervention" protocols reigned supreme: Forty hours a week of intense behavior training, speech therapy, and occupational therapy. Familiar, expected routines were overthrown. Leisurely trips to the park, spontaneous ice-cream excursions, and even naps were deposed in favor of rigid new protocols, color-coded schedules, and data tracking sheets. Stricken by the notion that our child's brain was rapidly cementing shut, there was no time for "normal" toddler activities. Urgent remediation became our new normal.

One afternoon, a behavioralist was working with Jeremy. At the time, our son had a maximum attention span of two seconds. While typical children might sit entranced by a puppet show or story time, my child was unable to attend to any instruction at all. Left on his own, he would spin and crash about all day like a little Tasmanian devil.

This session was particularly grueling. He began to tantrum in protest. Meanwhile, his mother languished on the sofa, recovering from a second miscarriage. In one room, a child bristled at sorely needed discipline administered by a trained professional. In another room, his physically and emotionally impaired mother lay emotionally paralyzed, lamenting their conjoined fate. What a sorry little lot we were.

As Jeremy thrashed and kept trying to flee the room, the therapist glanced up nervously. Should she press on? I hesitated. At age three, Jeremy was completely nonverbal. He was unable to express if he was hungry, in need, or in pain. Too bleary and conflicted to speak, I nodded. My darling little whirling dervish would not be permitted to remain this way. As the therapist swiveled around to continue, my son howled and implored with his eyes, *Why won't you fix this!*

Jesus Doeth All Things *Well*, Not *Easy*

From Jeremy's perspective, I did nothing to alleviate his misery. If anything, I idled by and callously endorsed his suffering. If Jeremy had been able to speak, he'd probably demand, "Why are you letting this happen? Don't you care? Why can't I eat, play, nap, and just live like any other three-year-old? It's not fair!"

This child had no idea how much I fiercely loved and desired the best for him. I knew why I was willing to subject him to all this. He desperately needed to be at a higher level of functioning than he was now. He could and must become so much more. But it would require considerable suffering and stamina—for all of us—to get there. I accepted and adored him, just as he was. But I loved him too much to leave him be.

There was also no way to adequately explain my intentions to him. His cognition was severely limited. Though he might misunderstand and even despise me, it wouldn't alter our plan for his development. He had no choice but to trust in my love and submit.

"Good Gifts"

> "If you, then, though you are evil, know how to give good gifts to your children, how much more will your Father in heaven give good gifts to those who ask him!"
> —Matthew 7:11

If I, in my compromised and weary state, knew how to have noble ambitions for my child, how much more so must my heavenly Father have a grander vision for me? God's ways are higher than ours (Isaiah 55:9). He defines blessing and good gifts differently. Good gifts are not limited to physical healing or any of our earthbound definitions of "blessing." Sometimes God's greatest gifts come wrapped in suffering.

I lay on the sofa feeling trapped and sorry for myself, like Jeremy. *Why is my life so hard? Why can't I have a normal pregnancy like other women? Why can't I have healthy children like everyone else? It's not fair!*

Instead of comparing and complaining, I needed to trust in my heavenly Father's heart and intentions for me. As Joni Eareckson Tada shares, "God permits what He hates to accomplish that which He loves."[7] He permits and repurposes hardship out of His great love. He has noble ambitions for His children to reach higher levels of functioning, too, be they spiritual, emotional, physical, or otherwise.

Though we may revile and resist the process, "God works for the good of those who love him, who have been called according to his purpose" (Romans 8:28). Discipline doesn't always mean punishment; sometimes it means training. Just as we insist on training and intensive intervention for our child's good, our heavenly Father trains us to strengthen *our* feeble faith and character. No discipline or hardship feels pleasant at the time. Later, however, it produces greater faith, conviction, strength, and capacity for those who have been trained by it (Hebrews 12:11).

Why does God allow our "torture"? Because, as Rick Warren wrote, "God uses pressure, heat, and time to create diamonds. In both rocks and people."[8] We are His beloved little Tasmanian devils. He accepts and adores us just as we are, spinning and crashing about in our sin and brokenness. Yet He loves us too much to leave us be. He intervenes and pursues us with an intense love, because He knows our potential to become so much more.

UNBREAKABLE PROMISES

- "So if you are suffering in a manner that pleases God, keep on doing what is right, and trust your lives to the God who created you, for he will never fail you" (1 Peter 4:19 NLT).
- "So take a new grip with your tired hands and strengthen your weak knees. Mark out a straight path for your feet so that those

who are weak and lame will not fall but become strong" (Hebrews 12:12–13 NLT).

- "And have you forgotten the encouraging words God spoke to you as his children? He said, 'My child, don't make light of the LORD's discipline, and don't give up when he corrects you'" (Hebrews 12:5 NLT).

Prayer

Lord, I claim Your promises in faith. "I consider that our present sufferings are not worth comparing with the glory that will be revealed in us" (Romans 8:18). Please help me to trust in Your perfect and noble intentions. I accept Your good gifts. I choose to submit to Your process to stretch and grow us to a higher ground of faith and ability.

Questions

1. How do you define a "good" gift? In contrast, how would God define a good gift?
2. Reflect on a previous season of trials. What unexpected "good gifts" or blessings came from them?
3. What situations do you wish God would fix? What is your perspective on discipleship through hardships? How can we trust in God's goodness despite feelings and circumstances that tempt us to conclude otherwise?
4. How is God disciplining and maturing you through your present struggles? What "harvest of righteousness" is being born through them? What good—"that which He loves"— is God accomplishing, by permitting that which He hates?

CHAPTER 11

"Why Won't God Intervene?"

CLOSE TO THE BROKENHEARTED

The righteous cry out, and the Lord hears them;
he delivers them from all their troubles.
The Lord is close to the brokenhearted and saves those
who are crushed in spirit. The righteous person may have
many troubles, but the Lord delivers him from them all.
Psalm 34:17–19

I hovered nearby, ready to intervene should the situation escalate. Jeremy had perched himself at the top of the playground slide, oblivious to the growing queue of children, irritated at being blocked from their turn. Sure enough, a gang of older boys began to protest. At best, autism made Jeremy oblivious to the complaints of others. At worst, it made him oblivious to the complaints of others.

He remained blissfully clueless to their pleas. Quizzical looks eventually turned into smirks and sidelong glances. They figured out *something's wrong with this kid.*

I sidled in closer, desperately hoping Jeremy would comply, or that those boys would cease. But the snickers devolved into mocking and taunting laughter. A feral protectiveness welled up in me, mama bear claws flicked open on instinct. I stood by on edge, tense and eager to annihilate the threat to my darling cub. But despite my thirst for blood, I willed myself to wait. With bated breath, I permitted my child's torment to continue.

Intervention!

Suddenly, a streak of orange appeared and flung himself between Jeremy and the menacing cluster. It was my younger son, Justin. His piping voice rang out across the playground, "You leave my brother ALONE! He has awe-tism!"

Just as I'd hoped, my four-year-old stormed in to ward off the pack of preteen predators. Taken aback by the kindergartener's bravado, the tween gang skulked and retreated from the playground. Mama bear claws retracting and blood pressure slowly ticking back to normal, I withdrew to my sentry post at the "mommy bench" a safe distance away and exhaled. The threat was neutralized.

Jeremy requires hypervigilance at all times. Because he has no sense of "stranger danger" or social awareness, my eyes can never leave him. I intervene often, but only when absolutely necessary. Not because I'm an uncaring or disengaged parent, but because I am an intentional one. My agenda? This precious, vulnerable babe must learn to stand up for himself. He needs to be equipped for the inevitable day he's bullied by a classmate—or worse, lured away by a predator.

Ten years of intensive speech therapy and countless episodes of "manufactured irritations" finally had trained Jeremy to say, "Stop it!" A decade of investment came to a head in this moment. Hence, I was loath to chopper in too soon, lest I rob him of the opportunity to exercise the self-advocacy skills he sorely needed.

I also wanted to test if Justin would come to his brother's aid. The laws of mortality had already ordained that I wouldn't always be around to intervene. Justin's training as lifelong guardian-in-waiting needed to begin sooner than later. Children cannot learn critical survival skills until parents hold back and let them.

Close to the Brokenhearted

No loving parent can bear to watch his or her children attacked. Our heavenly Father extends the same protective zeal over each of us. Whenever we face physical, spiritual, or emotional attack, He sidles in close. The Lord is near to the vulnerable, the oppressed, and the brokenhearted.

He summons a fleet of angels at the ready, and at just the right time, He deploys spiritual siblings as backup. Whether to distribute a miraculous supply of bread and fish, or to disseminate practical help and hope to a hurting world, He gifts His people with the opportunity to flex their compassion muscles—just one of many reasons He considers the "weaker" parts of the body indispensable (1 Corinthians 12:22).

Our fallen senses are quick to suspect that God leaves us alone in our struggles. But His eyes never leave His most vulnerable ones. He knows we require hypervigilance at all times and hovers near in stealth. He is our ever-present help in times of trouble. He is Emmanuel, God with us, who will never abandon nor forsake us.

He may not intervene immediately. Should He permit our struggle, it may be because He intends for us to acquire greater skills through the wait. Strength and resilience develop through testing and tension, not slack. Providence knows better than to undermine our spiritual growth by swooping in prematurely. Our Father desires for us to advocate and fight so that when the day of evil comes, we may be able to stand our ground (Ephesians 6:13).

UNBREAKABLE PROMISES

- "Yet Jerusalem says, 'The LORD has deserted us; the Lord has forgotten us.' 'Never! Can a mother forget her nursing child? Can she feel no love for the child she has borne? But even if that were possible, I would not forget you!" (Isaiah 49:14–15 NLT)
- "With all my heart I wait for the LORD to help me. I put my hope in his word" (Psalm 130:5 NIRV).
- "So be truly glad. There is wonderful joy ahead, even though you must endure many trials for a little while. These trials will show that your faith is genuine" (1 Peter 1:6–7 NLT).

Prayer

Jehovah-Shammah, You are the Lord who is there. You are present and near, even though I may not feel it. Help me to trust that when You don't deliver us immediately from trials, it is because You have higher purposes I may not understand. Help me to trust, surrender, and submit to the way You want to work in our lives.

Questions

1. Reflect on a time when your child was struggling. Did you intervene immediately or wait? Why? What wisdom or benefit was there to withholding immediate help?
2. Who are the spiritual siblings you can lean on for backup?
3. If He does not intervene immediately, what might He be up to instead? What might God be developing in you in the meantime?

CHAPTER 12

"Me? A Special-Needs Parent?"

LORD, PICK SOMEONE ELSE!

Moses said to the Lord, "Pardon your servant, Lord.
I have never been eloquent, neither in the past nor since you have
spoken to your servant. I am slow of speech and tongue."
The Lord said to him, "Who gave human beings their mouths?
Who makes them deaf or mute? Who gives them sight
or makes them blind? Is it not I, the Lord? Now go;
I will help you speak and will teach you what to say." But Moses said,
"Pardon your servant, Lord. Please send someone else."
Exodus 4:10–13

Like history is divided into BC and AD, so was our family narrative neatly bisected into two distinct eras: Before Autism and After. Before Autism, my hazy impression of special-needs parents was that they were a rare breed of human, noble souls preternaturally gifted with patience and oozing with otherworldly enlightenment. That's why God picked them. Ordinary persons were not worthy of so lofty a calling.

That is, until God picked me, a spectacularly less than average woman. Impatient and shrill, I once got so fed up at my child eating with his hands that I wrapped his fingers around a fork and sealed it into a fist with tape. Alarmed, my husband intervened and released our son before Child Protective Services found out.

Well-intended friends must have shared the same understanding because they attempted to encourage with "It takes a special person to raise a special-needs child." Only I didn't volunteer for this. I was drafted. The likes of me would never sign up for such an impossible gig, much less qualify. Perhaps that was the point. God was surely playing some cosmic joke with this epic mismatch of child to parent. It seemed a cruel irony to pair a vulnerable, delicate child with a reckless and feckless shrew like me.

Me, a special-needs parent? I'm not comfortable around disabled people. I avoid making eye contact. I'm irresponsible and lack empathy. I'm shallow, self-centered, and lazy. You've got the wrong person. Lord, please pick someone else!

It was as if God intentionally chose someone like me to demonstrate that He was God. And I was not.

I AM (and You Are Not)

"Who am I that I should go to Pharaoh and bring the Israelites out of Egypt?" (Exodus 3:11). Moses faced a daunting task. Anyone would have balked. Here was a man in midlife, who'd spent the last forty years in obscurity, tending to livestock. The desert of domesticity afforded plenty of alone time to ruminate over past mistakes. Suddenly, the Lord thrust him toward the courts of Pharaoh, the highest power in the land. Involuntarily conscripted to throw down a challenge before the ruler of the land and extract his labor force out from under his nose, Moses protested multiple times: he wasn't qualified. God agreed. Rather than inflate Moses's self-confidence by highlighting his princely upbringing or educational credentials, God reminded him, "I am who I am" (Exodus 3:14). He is God, and by deduction, Moses was not. The Lord's presence and power would be his sole asset to accomplishing the oversized assignment.

The Lord was fully aware Moses would require supernatural intervention to fulfill his calling. The Lord is not an unreasonable or hard master like Pharaoh. He does not require His people to build bricks yet withhold what they need to make them. Rather than setting them up for failure, God invites His people on a mission, positioning them to experience His enabling. At a conference, Henry Blackaby said, "The reality is that the Lord never calls the qualified; He qualifies the called."[9] Henry Blackaby expanded on this idea in his book, *Experiencing God*:

> He always matches His assignments with our character and faith in Him. . . . God is far more interested in accomplishing His kingdom purposes than you are. . . . As you obey Him, God will prepare you for the assignment that is just right for you. . . . Do not use human standards to measure the significance or value of His assignment. Whatever mission God gives, do it with all your heart.[10]

Moses's only requirement was obedience. As he stepped out in faith toward Egypt, God would provide the miracles. Faithfulness was Moses's job; fruitfulness was God's.

Who, Me? Yes, You

> Will God ever ask you to do something you are not able to do? The answer is yes—all the time! It must be that way, for

> God's glory and kingdom. If we function according to our ability alone, we get the glory; if we function according to the power of the Spirit within us, God gets the glory. He wants to reveal Himself to a watching world.
> —Henry Blackaby[11]

Does it require a special person to raise a child with special needs? No. It only requires a humble faith in an extraordinary God. God in His sovereignty saw fit to assign our unique child to us. Sometimes the most precious, personalized gifts are ineligible for return or exchange. There is no margin for "Please, pick someone else!"

Henry Blackaby wrote in his book *Created to Be God's Friend*, "'WHY NOW? WHY ME? WHY THIS?' These are phrases I hear constantly from those God is calling to Himself!"[12]

Through our journey of special-needs parenting, God draws us to Himself, so that we may tap into an immeasurable power of an almighty God. He promises to provide all we need to complete His assigned task. He is God; we are not. We need only expect Him to fulfill His role as we are faithful to ours.

Who am I that I should parent a child with delicate and complex needs? The only raw material we need to supply is our faith and obedience. Rather than fixate on our perceived lack, fix our eyes and anticipation on the One who specializes in making the impossible possible. Who gave humans their mouths, the gifts of speech, and sight? Was it not the Lord? Who created each of our children, fearfully and wonderfully made? Who decided on this divine pairing of child to parent and knit them unto us? Is it not the Lord? He will enable us to speak, to advocate, to raise, to bless this child, and to make him or her a blessing. In the book *Experiencing God*, Henry Blackaby wrote, "The truth is that God can do anything He pleases through an ordinary person who is fully dedicated to Him."[13]

The God of Moses also calls us to the "impossible" task of special-needs parenting so that we may demonstrate the greater power that is at work within us. In spite of our glaring inadequacy and lack, God will do what only a supernatural God can do. He is God. We are not.

It is His responsibility to assign, transform, provide, and deliver. He will provide what we need. He is faithful to His identity and responsibilities as the Great I AM. He asks us to be faithful to ours, as we parent our children and lead our families.

Now, go. Ten mighty miracles and more await.

UNBREAKABLE PROMISES

- "And my God will meet all your needs according to the riches of his glory in Christ Jesus" (Philippians 4:19).
- "If any of you needs wisdom, you should ask God for it. He is generous to everyone and will give you wisdom without criticizing you" (James 1:5 NCV).
- "Some trust in chariots, others in horses, but we trust the LORD our God" (Psalm 20:7 NCV).
- "But blessed are those who trust in the LORD and have made the LORD their hope and confidence" (Jeremiah 17:7 NLT).
- "I am the LORD, the God of all mankind. Is anything too hard for me?" (Jeremiah 32:27).

Prayer

Lord, I am not qualified for this daunting responsibility of raising a child with special needs. I am leaning on You to qualify and equip me for the calling You've given me. Fruitfulness and obedience are my responsibility. Fruit-bearing is Yours.

Questions

1. In what ways do you feel "unqualified" for special-needs parenting?
2. How is God stretching and shaping you to grow and overcome your shortcomings? How is He qualifying you for the call? What is one area where you can exercise stepping out in faith and obedience, despite feeling inadequate?
3. In what ways has God already proven that He is greater and more than sufficient to cover your inadequacies?

CHAPTER 13

"But I'm Not Qualified for This!"

UNSCHOOLED AND ORDINARY MEN

When they saw the courage of Peter and John and realized that they were unschooled, ordinary men, they were astonished and they took note that these men had been with Jesus. But since they could see the man who had been healed standing there with them, there was nothing they could say. So they ordered them to withdraw from the Sanhedrin and then conferred together. "What are we going to do with these men?" they asked. "Everyone living in Jerusalem knows they have performed a notable sign, and we cannot deny it."

Acts 4:13–16

As a child, those "handicapped" kids scared me. Tucked away in the portables at the rear of campus, it was as if they weren't meant to be seen. I tossed around the *R* word, never giving it a second thought. Retarded. Even as an adult, I avoided making eye contact with someone in a wheelchair. *Do I look or is that rude? Do they prefer I look away? Should I help with the door or is that condescending? Is it okay to say "handicapped"?* People with disabilities always made me nervous. Thinking about them took too much work. In public, I would swerve away in awkward haste to avoid running into them. I didn't know what to say or how to behave. Deep down, I didn't want to know. It was easier to simply avoid thinking about them at all.

Until my own child was diagnosed with autism. *Autism? I'm not qualified for this! This child needs a special-education teacher or a patient, homeschooling mom. I'm not cut out to raise a child with special needs.*

If I felt uncomfortable before, I was terrified now. Despite my having zero experience with disabilities, God assigned this child to me. This time, there was no way to avert my eyes. There would be no "take backs." This one was mine for keeps. Overwhelmed and underqualified, I felt trapped. Paired together, this fragile child and I were both doomed.

Great Commissions, Questionable Candidates

Throughout history, God has assigned Herculean-sized missions to the least likely candidates. The Author and Perfecter of our faith writes our story—His story—His way, hand-selecting a cast of His choosing. Ordinary folks can play a part in an extraordinary story.

Peter and John were unschooled, ordinary men. Their commencement into sainthood had inauspicious beginnings. In the immediate days following Jesus's crucifixion the disciples cowered in an upper room to regroup after the death of their beloved teacher.

Overwhelmed and trembling with fear, they must have wondered, *What do we do now?*

Jesus appeared to these unschooled and ordinary men with comfort and assurance. "Peace be with you!" (John 20:19). Unto them, raw and unpolished, the Holy Spirit came at Pentecost (Acts 2:1). To them, Jesus entrusted the lofty ministry of reconciliation. Upon them, God would build His church and the gates of Hades would not overcome it (Matthew 16:18).

Everyone knew their lack of credentials yet was astonished at their courage, boldness, and miraculous works. The disciples' one distinguishing feature was that they had been with Jesus. Evidently, spending intensive time with Jesus made a qualitative, transformative difference.

An Upper Room Convocation

Most of us didn't volunteer for special-needs parenting. We didn't seek out this life; it came to us. God understands our trepidation and fear. Even if we don't seek Him out, He comes to us to say, "Peace be with you!" Whether we're shivering behind a drafty configuration of fig leaves, locked down in an Upper Room, or holed up in a man cave somewhere, He knows we quake with fear and inadequacy.

To us, Jesus comes to comfort, assure, and reassure. He knows we feel acutely inadequate and unprepared for the assignment before us. Remember His preference for working miracles through underqualified people. Whatever our baseline may be, however un-credentialed, underqualified, or overwhelmed, do not underestimate what God can do. Our only certification is the certainty that comes through intensive time logged with Jesus.

The Holy Spirit Come upon You

When we spend real time with Him, we open ourselves to outstanding miracles, wonders, and signs our lives. Those familiar with our ordinary nature will notice our new, bold professions of faith. People in our towns and neighborhoods will witness a living miracle of transformation. Accredited by God, we will find ourselves deftly speaking IEP acronyms and languages we've never uttered. Enlightened in realms where we had no prior knowledge, we will boldly advocate where we once shrunk back in fear. There will be no denying, He will do it. Our Upper-Room convocation will be the commencement place of a calling.

UNBREAKABLE PROMISES

- "We are confident of all this because of our great trust in God through Christ. It is not that we think we are qualified to do anything on our own. Our qualification comes from God" (2 Corinthians 3:4–5 NLT).
- "For I can do everything through Christ, who gives me strength" (Philippians 4:13 NLT).
- "God began a good work in you. And I am sure that he will carry it on until it is completed. That will be on the day Christ Jesus returns" (Philippians 1:6 NIRV).
- "And He said to me, 'My grace is sufficient for you, for My strength is made perfect in weakness.' Therefore most gladly I will rather boast in my infirmities, that the power of Christ may rest upon me" (2 Corinthians 12:9 NKJV).
- "I will not be afraid, because the LORD is with me. People can't do anything to me. The LORD is with me to help me, so I will see my enemies defeated" (Psalm 118:6–7 NCV).

Prayer

Holy Spirit, come upon me. I'm terrified because I'm not qualified to adequately parent this child. I commit to leaning upon You, spending intensive time with You, and dwelling on Your promises. I pray for transformation that is evident to all. May transformation begin with me, that it would bless my child and ripple out as a witness to others.

Questions

1. What do you fear most about parenting your child with special needs? Call out your fears and name them.
2. Are you hiding out in fear or avoidance? How, where, and why?
3. Do you perceive God's voice of comfort seeking you out? In what practical ways can you respond?

CHAPTER 14

"I'm the Wrong Parent for This Child!"

OUR LIABILITIES LEVERAGED

For you created my inmost being; you knit me together in my mother's womb. I praise you because I am fearfully and wonderfully made; your works are wonderful, I know that full well.
Psalm 139:13–14

My mother sometimes laments My Loud Voice. When we are on the phone, she often asks me to turn down the volume or to speak farther away from the mouthpiece. She's perplexed how such a small woman (I stand less than five feet) can emit such a booming sound. Especially in the conservative Asian culture I come from, it's unbecoming for a girl to be brash. Loud daughters are a social liability.

Despite my mother's admonishment, I find myself having to use My Loud Voice regularly. I'm often shouting across a playground, a mall, or sometimes an entire city block. I do so to halt my child from bolting toward the street, completely unaware of oncoming traffic. He tends to walk ahead, oblivious to the rest of us trailing farther behind. Other times, it's to stop him from swiping french fries off a stranger's plate at a restaurant.

At six feet tall, my husband is also a booming presence. He, too, is forced to utilize his loud voice with our prone-to-wander child. Nevertheless, I usually need to intercede. His baritone often gets absorbed into the mass of people, muffled and ignored, whereas my shriek is much more effective at piercing through crowds to hail our son. With a will as fierce as my tone is shrill, My Loud Voice can slice through oceans to let me run through in hot pursuit of our child.

Liabilities, Leveraged

The Bible is full of brash, raw characters whose natural hardwiring got them into frequent trouble. The pre-Midian Moses, the pre-Peniel Jacob, the pre-Damascus Saul of Tarsus, and the pre-rooster Peter: each in their natural state may have suffered from a mild case of messiah complex. It took harsh failures for them to learn the hard way, that the job of Savior was taken. Moses was forced to endure a forty-year time-out in the desert before he would be redeployed to Egypt as a deliverer; Jacob was forced to declare spiritual bankruptcy and shed his hustler ways before he could become Israel; Saul had to be thrown off his misguided high horse before he could become the mighty apostle Paul; and Simon Peter's hubris had to get demolished before he could become Cephas, the rock on whom Jesus would build His church.

But what if Moses had steered clear of the burning bush? What if Jacob had tapped out prematurely from his wrestling match at

Mount Peniel? Or a blinded Saul refused to accept Ananias' offers of help? What if Peter remained mired in guilt and self-loathing? Time-outs can be timely; and tumblings, humbling. Once broken and bridled, God could reign in their natural impulses, and repurpose their passion into effective leadership for His people. They were converted and catapulted into greater service for the Lord.

Through surrender and obedience, through willingness to push through uncomfortable and undesirable circumstances, God can leverage our liabilities into assets for His kingdom.

We Are His Workmanship

I'm not the right person for this. I'm not patient enough. I'm not organized enough. I don't even like kids. I don't know anything about disability. I can't do this! God, pick someone else!

As special-needs parents, we are plagued by a chronic sense of "never enoughness." But God has hardwired each of us in unique ways that He repurposes to serve our children well.

After years gutted by insecurity and inadequacy, wracked by the sinking sense of "I'm not the right parent for this kid. He's doomed, paired with me," I came to appreciate My Loud Voice. He gave me this gift for a God-ordained reason. He knew I was going to need it to call my beloved, oblivious son home. To alert him of danger, to jolt his attention to a light that's gone red, or corral him back when we've turned left to his right.

The same Creator who custom-made my child also custom-fit *me*, Loud Voice and all. We are *both* wonderfully and fearfully made. A heavenly ordained pairing, we've been knit unto each other. *We*, together, are His workmanship. What God hath joined together, let no parent's self-doubt tear asunder.

In the classic film *Chariots of Fire*, Olympic runner Eric Liddell comes to accept his unique gifting and calling. After a time of struggle, he acknowledges, "I know God made me for a purpose. But He also made me fast, and when I run I feel His pleasure."

I, too, know God made me for a purpose. And when I am booming at my beloved son to call him home, I feel His pleasure.

UNBREAKABLE PROMISES

- "The LORD your God is in your midst, a victorious warrior. He will exult over you with joy, He will be quiet in His love, He will rejoice over you with shouts of joy" (Zephaniah 3:17 NASB).
- "When I consider your heavens, the work of your fingers, the moon and the stars, which you have set in place, what is mankind that you are mindful of them, human beings that you care for them? You have made them a little lower than the angels and crowned them with glory and honor" (Psalm 8:3–5).
- "No, despite all these things, overwhelming victory is ours through Christ, who loved us" (Romans 8:37 NLT).
- "This is my command—be strong and courageous! Do not be afraid or discouraged. For the LORD your God is with you wherever you go" (Joshua 1:9 NLT).

Prayer

Lord, You know everything about me, including the flaws that You can repurpose into assets. Help me to see the unique ways that You ordained this child unto me, and for me to be their parent. Together, we *are Your workmanship, conjoined to do good works in Christ, which You've prepared in advance for us to do.*

Questions

1. In what unique, "peculiar" ways has God hardwired you that bless and serve your child well? What liabilities can God leverage into assets?
2. What's the best surprise blessing your child has brought into your life?
3. How is God using special-needs parenting to mold you in your faith, character, and relationships?

CHAPTER 15

"But I Don't Want to Be Special"

HAVE TO VS. GET TO

From that day on, half of my men did the work,
while the other half were equipped with spears, shields,
bows and armor. The officers posted themselves behind
all the people of Judah who were building the wall.
Those who carried materials did their work with one hand
and held a weapon in the other, and each of the builders wore
his sword at his side as he worked. But the man who sounded
the trumpet stayed with me Then I said to the nobles,
the officials and the rest of the people, "The work is extensive
and spread out, and we are widely separated from each other along
the wall. Wherever you hear the sound of the trumpet,
join us there. Our God will fight for us!"

Nehemiah 4:16–20

Finding out your child has special needs is not like winning the lottery. Everyone wants their child to be special, but not *this* kind of special. "God gave you this child because He knew you could handle it" is a well-intentioned sentiment, as if being selected was a special honor. A complex disability like autism might happen to one in fifty, one in eighty-eight, or one in a hundred children. Statistics vary, but one truth remains constant: no parent ever wants their child to be *the one*.

Being different is undesirable. We'd prefer a once-a-year checkup with the pediatrician rather than multiple appointments a week. We'd prefer a child who whines, "Mommy, mommy, mommy!" endlessly rather than one who never speaks at all. We'd rather enjoy carefree outings and vacations instead of backup plans, exit strategies, and sudden aborts with profuse apologies as we back towards the door. Blending into the crowd at movies and restaurants is easier than fielding hostile stares and rude comments about our poor parenting. We wish attending church wasn't so complicated and difficult. We wish birthdays, graduations, and weddings were joyous occasions rather than bittersweet reminders of all that may never be for our own children.

No one wants to be "special" in this way. We would rather be ordinary, unexceptional, even humdrum so we could work, play, eat, and sleep like everyone else. No one rushes to pledge membership in this exclusive fraternity, the disabled community. Truth be told, many days we'd rather be dreadfully ordinary and unspecial—yes, "normal."

Divine Designation

In the book of Nehemiah, the prophet returned to Jerusalem to rebuild the devastated city. A gifted leader, Nehemiah deftly arranged the Judean reconstruction crew for strategic efficiency: half were positioned to defend from attackers, the other half focused on reconstructing the wall. But to one particular person, Nehemiah gave a unique responsibility: trumpeter. This trumpeter was to stand guard close to Nehemiah as a sentry, to summon the troops to battle in the event of attack.

As he took his position, separate from the others, and watched his countrymen labor in solidarity, I wonder if he felt isolated from their camaraderie. Did he resent his assignment, questioning, *Why me? Why do I have to do this, while everybody else gets to do that? Why can't I be like everyone else?*

Or, as the only man handpicked to stand nearest the commander, did he appreciate the gravity of his role? He alone was entrusted with the responsibility of alerting the company to danger. The safety and success of their mission depended on him. The trumpeter didn't have a choice in his assignment. He was picked. But he did have a choice in how he perceived it. Did he view his assignment as a dubious distinction or a divine designation?

From Other to Another

For special-needs families, the sense of "otherness" is pervasive. Different is a way of life. What comes easily for others—birthdays, restaurants, and holidays—is exponentially more difficult and complicated for us. It's human nature to desire acceptance and inclusion with the mainstream. We were designed for connection and community. But disability has a way of confounding our efforts. We long to fit in like everybody else, but "normal" now feels hopelessly out of reach. For us, normal has become the new weird.

I don't want to be special. Why me? Why us? Why do we get this while everybody else gets a normal life? Why can't we be like everyone else?

But had my child been like everyone else, I wouldn't have discovered how passionately I could love, how bitterly I could weep, how desperately I could pray, or how fiercely I could fight. Disability demolished my pride and self-sufficiency; it remapped the boundaries of my narrow mind—and even smaller heart—to greater expanses of sorrow, surrender, and submission.

Had we been like everyone else, I might not have passed through a refining fire that burned away the dross of complacency, shallowness, and self-centeredness. Suffering is a blaze that either purifies untested faith or melts it down and dissolves it completely.

Had we been like everyone else, the things that break God's heart might never have broken mine: valuing the devalued and seeking justice for the marginalized. In the words of Martin Luther King Jr., "Injustice anywhere is a threat to justice everywhere."[14] The discrimination that often accompanies disability inflamed an advocacy that spread beyond the special-needs community to embrace others relegated to outsider status. It ignited a newfound passion to speak up for those who cannot speak for themselves (Proverbs 31:8).

We did not have a choice in our assignment as special-needs parents, no more than Nehemiah's trumpeter did. But we can choose our attitude and perspective toward it; we can choose to incline our hearts and align our will with God's. Disability presents a unique opportunity to be molded, refined, and equipped. It is our divine distinction, an avenue for discipleship precious few have. We can resist, resent, and fight Him bitterly over our uncommon circumstances, or we can surrender and submit to His perfect sovereignty, "so that it will go well with us" (Jeremiah 42:6).

Have To Versus *Get* To

The world expects families like ours to be bitter, defeated, and joyless. Suffering primes us to become bitter . . . or better. In the face of chronic hardship, we have the opportunity to demonstrate how Jesus makes a difference. When we sacrifice to serve those whom the world deems unworthy; when we ascribe greater honor to those who lack it; when we face trials of many kinds but give thanks in all circumstances; when we manifest a peace the world does not understand, we command the attention of a cynical, startled world.

Our testimony is a clarion call: either we are lying, lunatics, or Jesus is truly Lord. When our lives demonstrate His strength made perfect in weakness, it points to a God who is tender, yet mighty to save. He is big enough to empower us through unrelenting pressures that break any ordinary person. Whether or not God "chose us because He knew we could handle it," He wants to accomplish the extraordinary through our children and families. When our human efforts run aground, the power of the Holy Spirit is the extra that differentiates between ordinary and extraordinary.

Special-needs parenting is an uncommon experience. Our children drive us to cling to Him daily with an unceasing desperation "normal" parents may never know. God invites us to stand nearest to Him, a privileged and unique vantage point. We're granted exclusive access to how deep the Father's love is for us, how vast beyond all measure.

Disability provides a rare angle for Him to demonstrate His power being made perfect through us. We may not build walls or brandish flashy swords as others do. We may not eat, sleep, work, play, or worship in conventional ways. Rather, we've been designated for a special purpose: to testify to a living God in peculiar, remarkable ways. Despite the threats and challenges we face every day, we've been issued an uncommon platform to broadcast before a watching world, "Our God will fight for us!" Our role and responsibility is to trumpet the name of God, to declare the glorious riches of Him who called us out of darkness—self-pity, a victim complex, a toxic sense of entitlement—and into His marvelous light.

So let others work, fight, and build in the normal ways. But us? It's not that we *have* to be special. It's that we *get* to be.

UNBREAKABLE PROMISES

- "For God is working in you, giving you the desire and the power to do what pleases him" (Philippians 2:13 NLT).
- "But now, thus says the LORD . . . 'Fear not, for I have redeemed you; I have called you by your name; You are Mine,'" (Isaiah 43:1 NKJV).
- "But you are a chosen people, a royal priesthood, a holy nation, God's special possession, that you may declare the praises of him who called you out of darkness into his wonderful light" (1 Peter 2:9).
- "We now have this light shining in our hearts, but we ourselves are like fragile clay jars containing this great treasure. This makes it clear that our great power is from God, not from ourselves" (2 Corinthians 4:7 NLT).

Prayer

Lord, please work in me to change my view. Help me see our unique experience as a special-needs family as a unique way to be discipled, and an uncommon means to testify to Your reality making a difference in our daily lives.

Questions

1. In what situations do you find yourself wishing, "Why can't we be like everybody else?" What can help you cope with this sense of "otherness"?
2. Do you view your child's disability as a dubious distinction, a divine designation, or both?
3. What unexpected blessings, experiences, or testimonies have emerged from "getting" to be a special-needs family?

CHAPTER 16

"Why Me? It's Not Fair!"

AN IEP FOR ME

"I tell you the truth, when you were young, you were able to do as you liked; you dressed yourself and went wherever you wanted to go. But when you are old, you will stretch out your hands, and others will dress you and take you where you don't want to go." Jesus said this to let him know by what kind of death he would glorify God. Then Jesus told him, "Follow me." Peter turned around and saw behind them the disciple Jesus loved—the one who had leaned over to Jesus during supper and asked, "Lord, who will betray you?" Peter asked Jesus, "What about him, Lord?" Jesus replied, "If I want him to remain alive until I return, what is that to you? As for you, follow me."

John 21:18–22 NLT

No mainstream parent accuses a special education parent of being "lucky." No one begrudges us or complains, "What about us? I want my child to be special too. It's not fair!" What is "fair"? Like many special-needs children, my son receives an Individualized Education Plan (IEP) at school.

At present, it includes a 1:1 shadow aide who supports him exclusively throughout the day, including speech therapy, occupational therapy, and behavioral therapy. Is it fair that my child gets a free bus ride to and from school while hundreds of other parents must jockey in the queue on a single-lane driveway to drop off their children? Is it fair that my child receives extra help at public expense, while other children must do their homework on their own and fend off bullies by themselves?

In consideration of the extraordinary challenges my child faces, there is implicit understanding that special treatment is only fair. Not only are these extras an approximation toward fairness, they are necessary for him to reach his goals and objectives. He cannot maximize his potential without them. Sometimes "unfair" accommodations or treatments are the only way to truly be fair.

"What about Me? It's Not Fair!"

When Peter asks Jesus, "What about him?" his underlying question is, "Why me? Why do I get it worse? It's not fair." On one level, perhaps it wasn't fair that Peter died upside down on a cross, while John enjoyed a relatively peaceful life and passed quietly from old age. Perhaps it wasn't fair that Jesus rebuked Peter harshly with, "Get behind me, Satan!" (Matthew 16:23) while John was "the disciple whom Jesus loved" (John 21:20).

But Peter was also the only human to ever walk on water, after the Son of God. When Satan asked to sift through all the disciples as wheat, Peter was the one disciple whom Jesus expressly prayed for, that his faith would not fail. Peter was the one Jesus appointed to encourage his brothers. Later, Peter was also the first apostle to enter the empty tomb of the risen Savior.

God had a specific calling and purpose for Peter: a highly individualized plan. God recognized the potential in Peter and faithfully led him to reach it. However, He also knew it might require extreme measures for this raw, volatile, and passionate Simon Peter, son of John, to be transformed into Cephas, the rock on whom Christ would build His church. Later beneficiaries of this church ought to give thanks that God didn't treat Peter fairly but implemented a unique plan for him instead.

Our experience with our children might feel like another chapter in unfairness. In the world of special education, a "fair and appropriate education" will look different for each child. It must. According to individual challenges and abilities, a customized plan is created to enable the child's learning. It's only fair. Some cognitively disabled children might need speech and behavior supports, while physically challenged students may need orthopedic accommodations. One size does not fit all. To insist on sameness wouldn't be fair.

It wasn't inappropriate that the Son of God should wash His disciples' feet, or permit an unclean woman to wash His.

It wasn't fair that a righteous man died a criminal's death, or that the condemned criminal received a last-minute reprieve to paradise. It's also unfair that children in developed nations receive help at the government's expense, while in darker corners of the earth, they are left to fend for themselves and die for lack of support.

Life is unfair, but God is just. He is merciful, full of grace and truth. Somehow, He will work out fairness in a way only a sovereign God can. When sinners with corrupted reasoning insist on fairness from a holy God, we know not what we ask. For all have sinned and fall short of the glory of God (Romans 3:23). For the wages of sin is death, but the gift of God is eternal life in Christ Jesus our Lord (Romans 6:23). Recipients of a death sentence have no right to demand the paper stock it comes written on. Let us not demand that God be "fair," but thank Him that He does not treat us as our sins deserve.

Spiritual IEP for Me

The Creator who knit each of us in our mothers' wombs and counts the hairs on our heads also knows the core deficits of our character and the deepest needs of our souls. In His providence, the Lord customizes a spiritual IEP for each of His children. He knows the plans He has for us, every test and failure we must persevere through to realize His ordained purposes for our lives. Each goal and objective He writes into our plan is perfectly accurate, fair, and appropriate. Unlike limited school-district budgets, His riches abound. He is faithful to supply all our needs in Christ Jesus, every accommodation and support we will need to maximize our potential.

God accommodated a young Mary's need to ask questions, but He punished Zechariah for asking why. To whom much is given, more is required. A priest should have known better. Jesus hastened to the home of Jairus to heal his daughter. But for the centurion's servant, His word alone was sufficient to heal from afar. Why? The centurion had demonstrated a faith unlike any Jesus had ever seen.

Why me? Why us? Why not them? Why not us? Through parenting a special-needs child, God permits the challenges He knows we need to optimally grow our character, faith, and witness. Through our striving to optimize our child's potential, our heavenly Father is working to optimize ours. The Lord has clearly indicated the kind of life by which we can glorify Him. Is it unfair compared to others who might have healthy children or "normal" family lives? He says to each of us as He said to Peter, "What about them? You must follow Me."

UNBREAKABLE PROMISES

- "That is why we never give up. Though our bodies are dying, our spirits are being renewed every day. For our present troubles are small and won't last very long. Yet they produce for us a glory that vastly outweighs them and will last forever! So we don't look at the troubles we can see now; rather, we fix our gaze on things that cannot be seen. For the things we see now will soon be gone, but the things we cannot see will last forever" (2 Corinthians 4:16–18 NLT).
- "But who are you, a human being, to talk back to God? 'Shall what is formed say to the one who formed it, "Why did you make me like this?"' Does not the potter have the right to make out of the same lump of clay some pottery for special purposes and some for common use?" (Romans 9:20–21).

Prayer

Lord, I've been comparing my life to others. It feels like everyone else has it easier. I've been discontent, complaining, and distracted by envy and bitterness. Please help me to focus on the work You desire to do in me, and the unique blessings You have in mind for my child.

Questions

1. In what areas are you tempted to compare your life with others? What feels "unfair" to you right now?
2. What are unique areas of weakness God might be working on? What goal, skill, or behavior is God working into your spiritual IEP?
3. In what ways is God speaking to you, "What about him/her/them? You must follow Me."

CHAPTER 17

"No One Understands!"

THE FELLOWSHIP OF OTHERNESS

Turn to me and be gracious to me, for I am lonely and afflicted.
Relieve the troubles of my heart and free me from my anguish.
Psalm 25:16–17

Every evening, my husband would return home to find children running amok, in various stages of undress. Toys and Tupperware littered the ransacked house. No comforting aromas of dinner greeted a weary man who worked long hours to put food on the table. Only the scent of neglect and indifference emanated from our cold and lifeless kitchen. Meanwhile, his disheveled wife sat stone-faced, pounding away at the computer. A frustrated and bewildered expression betrayed what his clamped lips knew not to ask. *What did you do all day?*

It was a mystery to both of us. Every day, I pedaled as hard as I could but got nowhere. I foraged all day but had nothing to show for it. My own husband couldn't understand. I couldn't understand, either, much less explain.

"You need to resubmit this application."

"I'm sorry, but this class isn't working for your child. He can't keep up with the other kids."

"Your insurance declined coverage again."

"You need to practice these exercises with him more often. Once a week isn't enough."

"We can't accept your child. He will have to wait-list."

Fruitless IEP meetings, phone calls and emails, a steady barrage of educational and therapeutic specialists merged into a mind-numbing blur of obligations. For every one item I managed to cross off my To Do list, five more cropped up to replace it. When everything is equally important and critically urgent, no one thing can be. Long days seeped into nights. Bleary and weary, I would collapse into bed until the next wave of demands pounded me awake. Every new morning, I woke up another six months behind.

What did I do all day? No one could understand. I couldn't understand either. "Nobody understands what I'm going through!" was partly true, and partly not. "If you've met one person with autism, you've met one person with autism" is a common aphorism in the world of autism spectrum disorders. Indeed, no one had our exact same set of circumstances, or the exact makeup and challenges as our son, especially when it came to a complex and highly individualized disorder like autism.

But I was not truly alone in my aloneness.

Only One Savior

In all of history, only one Person lays rightful claim to a unique experience no one else could understand. Royalty, radicals, and revolutionaries have come and gone with the ages. But the universe has known only one Savior. Only Jesus, who being in very nature God, left the glory of heaven to enter into a broken world.

No matter what misconceptions or unfair assumptions we may encounter, only Jesus endured lifelong judgment about His origins, identity, and intent—which ended His life. No matter how pressing our experiences may be, none of us have prayed so earnestly in anguish that our "sweat was like drops of blood falling to the ground" (Luke 22:44). No one drank the cup He drank. Only Jesus conquered death and the grave, rose, and was seated at the right hand of God, giving us hope for our present days and into eternity.

He alone best understands our feelings of otherness, alienation, and rejection. "He was in the world, and the world was made through Him, and the world did not know Him. He came to His own, and those who were His own did not receive Him" (John 1:10–11 NASB).

The cross of Christ trumps any claim to an exclusive pain. Because He has rightful ownership to this claim, He exercises the right to crash any pity party we might throw for ourselves. He has full access and authority to overturn our sorrows. "For we do not have a high priest who is unable to sympathize with our weaknesses, but we have one who in every respect has been tested as we are, yet without sin. Let us therefore approach the throne of grace with boldness, so that we may receive mercy and find grace to help in time of need" (Hebrews 4:15–16 NRSV).

He who best understands "No one understands!" invites Himself into our loneliness, so that we are no longer alone. When no one else can comprehend the load we carry, Jesus understands because He bore a solitary burden: the crushing weight of the sins of the world. When we feel invisible, unheard, and disregarded, He is our El Roi God who sees us, grieving alone in a relational desert (Genesis 16:13). He comforts, provides hope, and is the way for us to persevere.

The Solidarity of Solitude, the Fellowship of Otherness

Dreading that we were the only freak show in town, I searched online to connect with other special-needs parents. I discovered that our peculiar experiences weren't so isolated after all. Through faith-based support groups, virtual biblical encouragement, and ministries like Joni and Friends, I connected with other Christian parents of children with disabilities who also hungered for transcendent hope.

In *The Four Loves*, the great Christian apologist and author C. S. Lewis wrote, "Friendship is born at that moment when one man says to another: 'What! You too? I thought that no one but myself . . .'"[15] Just when I'd assumed I was the only one overwhelmed, misunderstood, and alone, I was deeply comforted to meet others who also contended with this unique grief, isolation, fatigue, and discouragement. They, too, felt overwhelmed and inadequate to manage the demands of special-needs parenting. We understood and "got" each other when no one else did. Despite a vast range of circumstances and conditions, we shared a universal sense of *otherness*. For once, we were no longer outsiders. In each other's company, we were *normal*.

Not Alone

Where does our help come from? It comes from the Lord, maker of heaven and earth (Psalm 121:1). Our struggles are not exclusive. No matter how rare a diagnosis, there is nothing new under the sun, even trials or heartache. The planet is littered with dark corners of suffering and injustice. In developing countries, disabled babies are rejected and abandoned, shriveled bodies are left to die on the street, women and children are trafficked and exploited. My first-world complaints are silenced before them. There will always be someone better or worse off. Neighboring together on a broken planet, we will encounter others with similar cuts, scrapes, and wounds to the heart. No one escapes the jagged edges of a broken planet unscathed.

No one but Jesus has the market cornered on isolation and suffering. Calvary silences all claims to an exclusive burden no one can understand. The Son of God endured a loneliness, isolation, and rejection that no one else ever will. He understands pain and punishment on a level we'll never know, because He bore them in our stead. No matter what we may go through, Jesus understands. Nothing compares to the help, hope, and empathy we find in Him.

God is with us and for us. He will turn and be gracious to us when we are lonely and afflicted. He will relieve the troubles of our hearts and free us from our anguish (Psalm 25:16–17). "So do not fear, for I am with you; do not be dismayed, for I am your God. I will strengthen you and help you; I will uphold you with my righteous right hand" (Isaiah 41:10).

He can lead us to others, to journey together so we don't have to travel alone. Allow God to direct your path to them. Seek and find them. Find community, even if virtually. He will bring people to come alongside us, to empathize, to understand, to know and be known. In the company of other "others" who've been struck down but not destroyed, we will discover that once we were not a people, but now we are the people of God.

UNBREAKABLE PROMISES

- "And let us consider how we may spur one another on toward love and good deeds, not giving up meeting together, as some are in the habit of doing, but encouraging one another—

and all the more as you see the Day approaching" (Hebrews 10:24–25).

- "Because he himself suffered when he was tempted, he is able to help those who are being tempted" (Hebrews 2:18).
- "This High Priest of ours understands our weaknesses, for he faced all of the same testings we do, yet he did not sin" (Hebrews 4:15 NLT).
- "For where two or three gather together as my followers, I am there among them" (Matthew 18:20 NLT).

Prayer

Lord Jesus, only You can lay claim to a truly unique burden that no one can understand. Other people face similar but different challenges as ours, but there is only one Savior. Please lead me to other special-needs families, so that we may connect and fellowship over our shared otherness. Please help me to conclude that with You, we are never really alone.

Questions

1. What unique challenges do you face that you wish others understood better?
2. What can you do to fight feelings of isolation or loneliness? Who or where is your safe place?
3. In what unexpected ways has God shown that He sees you (El Roi God)? How has He demonstrated His ever-present care for you?
4. Have you connected with other special-needs parents who "get" what you're going through? If not, what might be your next step to connect with others?

CHAPTER 18

"Sit with Me, for I Am Overwhelmed"

COMPASSION: SUFFERING WITH

They went to a place called Gethsemane, and Jesus said to his disciples, "Sit here while I pray." He took Peter, James and John along with him, and he began to be deeply distressed and troubled. "My soul is overwhelmed with sorrow to the point of death," he said to them. "Stay here and keep watch." Going a little farther, he fell to the ground and prayed that if possible the hour might pass from him. "Abba, Father," he said, "everything is possible for you. Take this cup from me. Yet not what I will, but what you will." Then he returned to his disciples and found them sleeping. "Simon," he said to Peter, "are you asleep? Couldn't you keep watch for one hour? Watch and pray so that you will not fall into temptation. The spirit is willing, but the flesh is weak." Once more he went away and prayed the same thing. When he came back, he again found them sleeping, because their eyes were heavy. They did not know what to say to him.

Mark 14:32–40

Let me know if you need anything."

"I don't know how you do it. I couldn't handle all that."

"Just pray and trust God. Your child will turn out fine. Just have faith."

"Have you tried ______?"

Friends, family, and fellow believers—all with the best of intentions—sometimes express comments more hurtful than helpful. Or they may withdraw, intimidated, shushed into silence for fear of getting it wrong. Because they often don't know what to say or do, their intended blessings can often result in inadvertent bruising. There's no way to win in supporting a family struggling with disability, it would seem.

Or is there?

Divine Dependence

At the garden of Gethsemane, Jesus struggled as He prepared for His final hours. Deeply distressed, He sought the support of His three most trusted friends—friends who would ultimately disappoint when their physical fatigue outweighed their devotion to the Lord.

But what could these friends have said? What could they have possibly done to help? Peter's previous attempts to exhort, "Never, Lord! . . . This shall never happen to you!" (Matthew 16:22), or affirm at the Transfiguration (Mark 9:5–6) only backfired disastrously. No feeble words of encouragement could have changed an unchangeable situation. There was no opting out of Jesus's mission, no bypassing or mitigating His suffering to come. What could any mere human have done to alleviate the burden of the Lamb of God, who had come to take away the sins of the world? Jesus's burden was His alone to carry.

Even Jesus, being in very nature God, needed the emotional

support of friends to sit with Him in His darkest hour. He needed physical help when His human strength failed en route to His own death. Simon of Cyrene was forced to carry Jesus's cross when He could carry it no farther (Luke 23:26). Because Jesus was fully human in every way, He faced every temptation and trial known to humanity: misunderstanding, judgment, betrayal, abandonment, loneliness, isolation, and the utter depletion of strength. While being omnipotent and divine, He also experienced being overwhelmed and dependent.

And we judge Him not for it.

Compassion, the Art of Suffering With

"I'm going to Target on Thursday. Can I pick up stuff for you?"

"How's it going? Can I take you out for ice cream? My girls can watch your kids."

"I want to come over and play with the kids. Let's schedule a date night."

"Tell me how I can help. I don't know what to do but I want to. Help me help you, because I'm not going away."

"I'm praying for you. No need to reply if you're overwhelmed. Just know you're loved."

Despite hurtful comments or slights we've sustained, we've also been blessed by thoughtful friends who expressed sublime words of comfort and specific offers of help. They've offered up a listening ear, sympathetically receiving my ravings with a refreshing absence of judgment or admonishment to behave "more spiritual." Rather than offer advice or even memory verses, mercifully, they let us do the talking. Wise friends come ready to hold an emotional barf bag for us. Let the heartsick people fill the bag. They've also ambushed us with bags of groceries, delivered meals, kidnapped me for "mandatory" pedicures, and kept watch over our children when our patience had long been depleted.

The etymology of compassion is "co-suffering," to suffer with. Supportive friends have demonstrated compassion *for* me, as they sat and suffered *with* me. Our friends may not be able to carry our unique burdens for us. But they can carry *us*.

We were not meant to struggle, overwhelmed and alone. Our Father has always known it is not good for us to be alone (Genesis 2:18). God created us to be in Christ-centered community. He desires to dispatch help and comfort through others. "Is anyone among you in trouble? Let them pray. Is anyone happy? Let them sing songs of praise. Is anyone among you sick? Let them call the elders of the church to pray over them and anoint them with oil in the name of the Lord" (James 5:13–14).

Special-needs parenting is too heavy a burden to carry alone. A burden shared is a burden divided. When our souls are overwhelmed with sorrow, stress, and anxiety, we must seek out safe places and lean on safe people. Even though we risk disappointment, we must be humble and willing to be known. Jesus wasn't too proud to seek support and encouragement. He who carried a burden no one could understand leaned on the compassion and fellowship of well-meaning yet flawed men. Vulnerability involves risk, requiring humility and strength.

Our Lord lived by this example. If even the Son of God humbly relied on the support and strength of others, how much more so should His earthly children. Where Peter, James, and John had failed Jesus, my helpful friends Cindy, Janice, Delia, and Gisele succeeded. Overwhelmed parents are chronically in need of compassionate friends to be with us, to sit with us and keep watch. The lifelong squeeze of special-needs parenting leaves little room for motherhood martyrdom. There is only one Savior; His name is Jesus. We must be willing to accept, and even ask for, help. It's what Jesus would do, what He has done, and what He desires we follow in His footsteps.

UNBREAKABLE PROMISES

- "Cast all your anxiety on him because he cares for you" (1 Peter 5:7).
- "Two people are better off than one, for they can help each other succeed. If one person falls, the other can reach out and help. But someone who falls alone is in real trouble" (Ecclesiastes 4:9–10 NLT).
- "I lift up my eyes to the mountains—where does my help come from? My help comes from the LORD, the Maker of heaven and earth" (Psalm 121:1–2).
- "He will rescue the poor when they cry to him; he will help the oppressed, who have no one to defend them" (Psalm 72:12 NLT).

Prayer

Lord Jesus, even You needed reliable and supportive friends to lean on. I do too. Please help me be humble and vulnerable about sharing my need for help. I pray You send safe, compassionate friends willing to sit, pray, and suffer with us. Give me eyes to recognize those You are preparing.

Questions

1. What well-intended clichés, unhelpful comments, or unintended slights have you endured? What do you wish had been said or done instead?
2. Who do you have to "sit and keep watch" with you? To walk alongside, support, and pray for you?
3. Why is it difficult to accept help—much less ask for it—even when we are legitimately overwhelmed? How might God be challenging that resistance?
4. What might be the next step in establishing a support network for you, emotionally and practically? What's the next best thing you can do?
5. What would be your dream list for practical help? Write down your secret wish list. Prayerfully consider sharing the list with trusted friends or family who desire to help but may not know how.

CHAPTER 19

"Is This It? Or Should We Expect Something Else?"

JESUS, PLUS

When the men came to Jesus, they said, "John the Baptist sent us to you to ask, 'Are you the one who is to come, or should we expect someone else?'" At that very time Jesus cured many who had diseases, sicknesses and evil spirits, and gave sight to many who were blind. So he replied to the messengers, "Go back and report to John what you have seen and heard: The blind receive sight, the lame walk, those who have leprosy are cleansed, the deaf hear, the dead are raised, and the good news is proclaimed to the poor. Blessed is anyone who does not stumble on account of me."

Luke 7:20–23

In the summer of 1967, an athletic teen dove headfirst into the Chesapeake Bay for a swim. A devastating miscalculation of the water's depth resulted in the girl striking her head on the bottom, snapping her neck. Later, as she lay permanently paralyzed in her hospital bed, flipped every two hours to stare between floor and ceiling, she vacillated between praying for healing and pleading for death.

Was this it? At the tender age of seventeen, was she resigned to quadriplegia and despair? In the face of irreparable damage to her spinal cord, healing appeared an unrealistic expectation. Disabled in body and crippled in spirit, she cried out to the God she thought she knew, "God, I can't . . . I can't live like this. If You won't let me die, then please show me how to live!"[16]

Family and friends came to pray and encourage. But many would graduate and move on to build careers and families of their own. Meanwhile, enveloped in the dark confines of her bedroom, she watched the seasons pass by. Would God deliver her from imprisonment in a lifeless body, chained to a hopeless future? Was this it, or should she expect something more?

What Should We Expect?

John the Baptist had been faithful. Then, after fulfilling his assignment as the forerunner for the Messiah, he found himself in an unlikely position: imprisoned. For all his efforts, this servant of God was rewarded with the threat of death. Meanwhile, others were being healed and experiencing Jesus's healing. The blind were regaining sight, the deaf could now hear . . . Surely John must have wondered, *What about me?* Chagrined at his fate, he dispatched his disciples to inquire of Jesus, "Are you the one who is to come, or should we expect someone else?" (Luke 7:20). Jesus could have saved John, but He didn't. The Great Deliverer wasn't delivering according to John's disciples' expectations. They were assured of Jesus's identity but unnerved by His lack of intervention. They were troubled not by the radical things Jesus was doing, but by the things He was *not* doing.

John would remain in prison and die the gruesome death of a

martyr. Yet Jesus offered this public commendation, "Among those born of women there is no one greater than John" (Luke 7:28). Evidently, a call to greatness doesn't exempt the commended one from suffering.

Jesus, Plus

Disappointment has a way of dredging our unspoken expectations to the surface. When a dreaded diagnosis is confirmed, Jesus hasn't complied with our expectations of a "good God." If God is good, how could He permit this? We feel betrayed by a God who disregards our earnest prayers and wishes. Perhaps He can't be trusted after all. Instinctively, we retreat to a corner to nurse our spiritual wounds.

Subconsciously, we had expected Jesus, *plus*. We knew salvation through Christ guaranteed our eternity in heaven. But somehow, we assumed comfort and ease came bundled as an all-inclusive package. We defined "blessing" on our own terms and felt cheated at encountering pain and injustice instead.

The Savior delivers us from the penalty and power of sin. Jesus reconciles our separation from God and ushers us into a life of hope and purpose. God is able to heal and miraculously deliver. But the Bible never promised us that a life of faith would be exempt from suffering. Nowhere does it guarantee us a free pass from pain. The outcomes of John the Baptist and all the saints of old chronicled in the "hall of faith" of Hebrews chapter 11 underscore the surrender of expecting fulfillment in this lifetime.

> All these people were still living by faith when they died. They did not receive the things promised; they only saw them and welcomed them from a distance, admitting that they were foreigners and strangers on earth. People who say

> such things show that they are looking for a country of their own. If they had been thinking of the country they had left, they would have had opportunity to return. Instead, they were longing for a better country—a heavenly one. Therefore God is not ashamed to be called their God, for he has prepared a city for them. . . . These were all commended for their faith, yet none of them received what had been promised, since God had planned something better for us so that only together with us would they be made perfect.
> —Hebrews 11:13–16, 39–40

Foreigners and strangers to earth rest assured in their heavenly citizenry. They know the American Dream is but a provincial one. This is what the ancients were commended for. Our child's disability offers us a unique opportunity to flex the same faith. We may be perplexed at what Jesus is not doing, but not despairing. We may be struck down and disappointed by the loss of unmet expectations, but we are not destroyed (2 Corinthians 4:9).

A Proper Place of Healing

The seventeen-year-old quadriplegic teen of 1967 was Joni Eareckson Tada. Today, she is founder and CEO of Joni and Friends, an international ministry for the disabled, author of over fifty books, guest on countless radio programs and interviews, and inspirational speaker to audiences across the world. She stands as a modern-day hero of the faith, while remaining seated in her wheelchair.

"My wheelchair was the key to seeing all this happen—especially since God's power always shows up best in weakness. So here I sit . . . glad that I have not been healed on the outside, but glad that I have been healed on the inside." [17]

Joni can be thankful for her wheelchair, just as Apostle Paul was thankful for his imprisonment in chains that served to advance the gospel (Philippians 1:12). Quadriplegia, imprisonment, and disability are all unexpected "disappointments" an almighty God can redeem.

"Permanent" disability is but fleeting until we meet full healing at the resurrection; so is our temporary spiritual paralysis and crisis of faith. We may feel off put when God doesn't alter our circumstances according to our wishes. But if God is not changing our circumstances on the outside, then He is working to change us on the inside. Joni writes, "A no answer has purged sin from my life, strengthened my commitment to Him, forced me to depend on grace, bound me with other believers, produced discernment, fostered sensitivity, disciplined my mind, taught me to spend my time wisely, and widened my world beyond what I would have ever dreamed had I never had that accident in 1967."[18]

God may heal our children; He may not. Victory and deliverance may also come in unimaginable ways, as they did for Joni. From Hebrews 11, to John the Baptist, to Paul imprisoned, to Joni Eareckson Tada, our unfulfilled expectations present us opportunities to stand in esteemed company. Our story can become an additional chapter in God's glorious anthology of faith.

Like John's disciples, we may witness other people's children make further progress. Like Joni, we may watch others develop, move on to independence, and build families of their own, while our children do not. God may even heal their children but not ours. Should we expect something more, something else? Yes and no. Let us surrender our expectations of how God should bless or deliver us. He is who He says He is. We should not expect any other Savior or salvation.

We *can* expect our Savior to redeem and repurpose our

disappointments. In God's sovereignty, He will administer blessing and healing in ways that are far higher. Is this it? Or should we expect something else? We should expect Him who is able to do immeasurably more than we could ask or imagine, according to His power that is at work within us (Ephesians 3:20).

In the meantime, go back and report what you see. Quadriplegics establish international ministries, mothers of children with autism write books; some receive miraculous healings, while others testify to "healing on the inside." Lives are transformed, and faith is revived while bodies remain impaired. "Blessed is anyone who does not stumble on account of me" (Matthew 11:6).

UNBREAKABLE PROMISES

- "Let us draw near to God with a sincere heart and with the full assurance that faith brings, having our hearts sprinkled to cleanse us from a guilty conscience and having our bodies washed with pure water. Let us hold unswervingly to the hope we profess, for he who promised is faithful" (Hebrews 10:22–23).
- "Even though the fig trees have no blossoms, and there are no grapes on the vines; even though the olive crop fails, and the fields lie empty and barren; even though the flocks die in the fields, and the cattle barns are empty, yet I will rejoice in the LORD! I will be joyful in the God of my salvation" (Habakkuk 3:17–18 NLT).
- "These were all commended for their faith, yet none of them received what had been promised, since God had planned something better for us so that only together with us would they be made perfect" (Hebrews 11:39–40).
- "Now faith is the substance of things hoped for, the evidence of things not seen" (Hebrews 11:1 NKJV).

Prayer

Lord, I confess I had expected Jesus, plus. I wasn't even aware of these expectations imbedded into my beliefs, until disability unearthed them. You are able to deliver and heal. Teach me to expect that You will do immeasurably more than I could ask or imagine, according to Your promises. Your will may include physical healing for my child; and it may not. But You guarantee spiritual healing and reconciliation for those who seek it. You are enough, Lord Jesus. I desire to experience You as El Shaddai, the all-sufficient One.

Questions

1. What other "plus" benefits, in addition to salvation, did you expect? What unspoken expectations do you now feel disability excludes you from?
2. What other purposes or "places of healing" might God be working to deliver in your life?
3. How might God be repurposing your "pluses" or idealized expectations to experience that which only He can deliver? Where is God trying to redirect your attention—new blessings you may be unable to recognize—due to your insistence on the pluses?

CHAPTER 20

"Never, Lord!"

WHEN GOD WON'T BEHAVE

Peter took him aside and began to rebuke him.
"Never, Lord!" he said. "This shall never happen to you!"
Jesus turned and said to Peter, "Get behind me, Satan!
You are a stumbling block to me; you do not have in mind
the concerns of God, but merely human concerns."
Matthew 16:22–23

Mac and cheese, Goldfish crackers, and pasta: the quintessential staples of a toddler diet. Our toddler was no different. Until autism came. Like any parent desperate for a cure, we were willing to try anything that might help, including a gluten-free, casein-free diet.

Out went all our son's favorite crackers and snacks, and in came a laundry list of stringent dietary restrictions. Milk and ice cream were forbidden, with gummy and tasteless substitutions only highlighting his deprivation. All favorite treats were dumped with no explanation. How could a nonverbal three-year-old comprehend the gastrointestinal intricacies of leaky gut syndrome or intestinal hyperpermeability? I didn't bother to explain.

Truthfully, it meant more mindfulness and stress for me than for him. I was forced to maintain near-kosher standards of separation in our kitchen to keep his food from being contaminated by the rest of the family's. Finding substitutions required extensive Internet searches and intricate meal planning. Gluten-free, casein-free alternatives were also twice as costly. On trips to the supermarket, he caught on to my hasty attempts to bypass the snack aisle. He would have none of it and made his feelings known. *"TEEEEEETOOOOOOHHHH!" Teeeeeeeetoooooh!"*

Lacking appropriate speech, he defaulted to his preferred means of communication, screaming nonsensical words. He had just witnessed his mother speeding away from his favorite aisle. Clearly, she had no intention of replacing his favorite foods. His deepest suspicions had been confirmed: I was the meanest mother in the world. This woman could no longer be trusted.

The False Gospel of "Never, Lord!"

In Matthew 16, Jesus revealed to His disciples His coming suffering, death, and resurrection. Peter's reaction expressed his extreme displeasure with Jesus's approach to Messiah work. "Never, Lord! . . . This shall never happen to you!" (v. 22). Peter's outburst exposed an adherence to a gospel of his own invention, one diametrically opposed to the Lord's. Outright rejection of God's authority was serious business, worthy of sharp rebuke.

"Get behind me, Satan! You are a stumbling block to me . . ." (v. 23).

Jesus was swift to stamp out Peter's errant ideas of how the Savior should save. The most effective way to straighten Peter out was to point out sharply where he was wrong. It was urgent and imperative that he who held the keys to the kingdom (Matthew 16:19) build upon a foundation of sound doctrine.

If Peter couldn't argue the cross out of Jesus's calling, we ought not negotiate it out of ours. Let us rebuke that within us which revolts against the suffering that yields our sanctification. Let us renounce false gospels that pose stumbling blocks to our discipleship.

"God helps those who help themselves."

"If you're faithful, God will bless you."

"Name it and claim it! Pray and God will answer your prayers."

"No. This shall never happen to me!"

When scripture states emphatically that we did nothing to cause our child's disability (John 9:1–3), no human machinations can un-cause it. No magical prayer, mystical incantation, or quid pro quo can manipulate God into giving us what we want. The great Almighty is not a cosmic vending machine, genie, or lucky charm. He is not beholden to move or to act as mere mortals wish. A god who bends to the whims and demands of mere mortals is no god at all. A gospel that promises prosperity and blessings in exchange for tokens of sacrifice is bankrupt; it is no gospel at all (1 Samuel 15:22).

Our Holiness Versus Happiness

Children often cry out for their parents to give in to their desires. They lack understanding that sometimes, a parent's duty is not to appease but to oppose. Greater love may require the denial of a beloved child's dearest wish. Prioritizing the child's best interests is paramount to the parent's reputation. Mature and loving parents are willing to risk being misunderstood and even despised to do what's best for their children.

Our children are God's greatest gifts to us. "God always gives his best to those who leave the choice with him."[19]

But like Peter, we may react violently against the way God decides to bless us. *Who, me? A special-needs parent? Never, Lord! This is not how You're supposed to work. This is not how it's supposed to be!* In our hearts, we pull Him aside and reproach Him. But He is God; we are not. Despite our cries of protest and demands for deliverance, our heavenly Father remains steadfast in His commitment to our holiness over our happiness. He will always prioritize eternal consequences over our short-term satisfaction. So great the Father's love for us, He was willing to pay the ultimate price.

God is willing to risk being misunderstood, and even risk our ire, to secure our eternal well-being. He refuses to settle for anything less. Neither should we refuse to settle for anything apart from His will for us. As immature children, we see our lives from a worldly perspective, where blessings are defined by comforts, pleasure, and achievement. Our world would hardly consider disability a blessing. Such perspectives are of the minds of men, not God.

When God doesn't behave according to our expectations of a "blessed" life, we often react violently, like Peter. He could not accept that the Savior should suffer. We can't accept that His followers should either. In our inability to view lordship and our discipleship from God's perspective, we lash out at Him for not conforming to our earthly expectations of how He should be.

Man seeks comfort and deliverance from suffering. God seeks our holiness. Through Jesus, we have evidence of how suffering, surrender, and submission become the pathway to peace.

We may not have had a choice in how our children were born.

But we do have a choice in how we respond. When we release our grip from tightly held notions of how God should be and what He should do for us—the rights and blessings we insist are ours—we can experience the full measure of all God intended.

Let us surrender our insistence of how the Savior ought to save, and our faulty notions of how He ought to work in our lives. As Joni Eareckson Tada wrote in her book *Joni: An Unforgettable Story*, "Only God is capable of telling us what our rights and needs are. You have to surrender that right to Him."[20]

God is God, and we are not. Let Him define what is good, what is a blessing. When we pivot from "Never, Lord!" to "May it be to me as You have said" (Luke 1:38), we hold unswervingly to the hope we profess, for He who has promised is faithful (Hebrews 10:23). In this way, we exalt the things of God in our lives, above the things of men.

UNBREAKABLE PROMISES

- "For my thoughts are not your thoughts, nor are your ways my ways, says the LORD. For as the heavens are higher than the earth, so are my ways higher than your ways, and my thoughts than your thoughts" (Isaiah 55:8–9 NRSV).
- "How terrible it will be for anyone who argues with their Maker! They are like a broken piece of pottery lying on the ground. Does clay say to a potter, 'What are you making?' Does a pot say, 'The potter doesn't have any skill'?" (Isaiah 45:9 NIRV).
- "Then Job replied to the LORD: 'I know that you can do all things; no purpose of yours can be thwarted. You asked, "Who is this that obscures my plans without knowledge?" Surely I spoke of things I did not understand, things too wonderful for me to know'" (Job 42:1–3).

Prayer

Lord, Your purposes and ways are higher than I can imagine. Your greater purposes can quell my anger at not getting the life I expected. Forgive me for limiting You and making a god of my own image. You are committed to my holiness, more than my happiness. In becoming more like You, there is true joy and peace that surpasses understanding. As You are committed, please help me be committed to pursuing holiness too.

Questions

1. Are you committed to holiness over happiness? Do you insist on how Jesus should save or deliver you, or surrender to His higher purposes?
2. How is God repurposing your struggles to mold you into the image of Christ? How does suffering aid the process of sanctification?
3. What is an example of having every worldly comfort or luxury but lacking eternal peace and significance? Conversely, recall a prior experience of personal hardship or suffering that was paradoxically marked by the joy and transcendent peace of Christ.

CHAPTER 21

"What Has Happened to Me . . . ?"

LIFE, HIJACKED AND IMPRISONED

Now I want you to know, brothers, that what has happened to me has really served to advance the gospel.

Philippians 1:12

As a starry-eyed college student, I daydreamed over which impressive acronyms might follow my name on a business card someday: PhD, MD, JD, Esq. When I became a Christian, I transferred those ambitions into accomplishing even greater things for the kingdom of God. With the drive and creative passions God bundled me with, many were the plans in this young woman's heart.

Then, autism happened.

"So, what do you do?"

"Nothing. I'm just a stay-at-home mom."

Suddenly, I was "just" a mom. The ignoble acronym "SAHM" became my humble handle. Parenting little ones is a grueling and often thankless task. But caring for a child who perennially functions at the level of a toddler is extreme parenting. For parents like us, the finish line isn't watching our child victoriously cross the threshold of adult independence. Ours is an unrelenting slog toward our own expiration date: death. I was bound to a child who would need me forever. Parents of typical youngsters are often reassured, "This is just a season. It all goes by so quickly." But for parents of children with lifelong disabilities, the season expires only when we do.

Domestic drudgery was a far cry from the accomplished life I'd envisioned. The sky was the limit, until the ceiling fan needed dusting. All the great and glorious things I wanted to do, I no longer could. The mundane and monotonous I did not want to do, I had to keep doing.

Stifled and trapped, a new mantra looped in my mind, *I'm not supposed to be stuck here like this. This is not what I'm supposed to be doing with my life. How could God let this happen to me? You've got the wrong person cooped up in here! There must be some mistake . . .*

All my dreams for our family had been hijacked. As much as I grieved the loss of potential for my child's future, I also grieved the loss of mine. Years of education, training, and hustle to see aspirations fulfilled were wasted, a write-off. Why nurture lofty yearnings only to shelve them? What has happened to us? What could happen to us? How could our dreary existence possibly advance the gospel?

Convictions Held Captive

Throughout the New Testament, few demonstrated upward spiritual mobility like Apostle Paul. Formerly a notorious persecutor of the first-century Christians, his dramatic conversion transformed him into the church's most ardent advocate. His illustrious ministry spanned three missionary journeys, multiple church plants, and countless new converts.

Then, a sudden hijacking of plans: his brilliant trajectory was abruptly cut short. At the peak of his career, *"What has happened to me"* included multiple imprisonments, languishing in jail, and ultimately dying a martyr's death. Paul had earthly reason to feel bewildered and chagrined. The sudden curtailing of his vibrant ministry could have felt like a cosmic tragedy. Why ignite such fiery passion for expansion of the gospel, only to snuff it out in a dank dungeon? Few were as elite in background, natural in gifting, and uniquely positioned for impact like Paul. Why such waste?

But Paul knew the secret to being content in any circumstance. In *Life Principles from the New Testament Men of Faith,* the authors summarize key insights from the book of Philippians, chapter 1, about Paul's imprisonment:

> First, we learn that his negative circumstances brought the positive result of further advancement of the gospel (v. 12). Secondly, we are told that those circumstances opened the whole Praetorian Guard to the gospel (v. 13). Third, we discover that the brethren trusted the Lord because of Paul's imprisonment and that the brethren had more courage to speak the word without fear. Finally, we learn that through Paul's imprisonment, Christ was exalted (v. 20).
>
> Paul had learned something important about prisons—God makes our prisons into our pulpits. If God has placed us in a prison, then that is where He wants to use us. Paul had already seen that at work. He was so focused on God

> that instead of moaning about his lost freedom, or complaining of his dire circumstances, he rejoiced that his going to prison had turned out, ". . . for the greater progress of the gospel." His focus was not on his suffering, but on how many people his sufferings had brought into his life for the sole purpose of ministry. Because of the essence of his life was Christ, Paul could have the same attitude of humility that Christ had. We can also have that same attitude today.[21]

Because Paul surrendered to God's agenda, God could repurpose Paul's prison into a pulpit. A dungeon became the desktop from which Paul composed his greatest legacy: letters that became thirteen books that now comprise the bulk of the New Testament.

Penned for a Purpose

Few in Paul's day were qualified or had the pedigree, much less the focus and intensity required, to pen thirteen books. Only an omniscient God knew to redeploy a passionate Paul from entrepreneurial ministry to the solitary work of a scribe. This sudden, inexplicable redirect would bless countless future generations. Today, we are beneficiaries of Paul's submission to the mysterious ways of God.

Paul was able to view his suffering through the lens of faith. He acknowledged "what has happened to me" was for the advancement of the gospel, while having no inkling or interest of his future status as author and one of history's greatest champions of the faith. His eternal contributions were enabled by his earthly captivity. The temporary chains of that one unlocked eternal freedoms for many. Paul's imprisonment unleashed the robust expansion of the gospel. Under

God's redemptive hand, closed doors can lead to new opportunities; the demise of old passions can birth new purposes.

Hallowed Hijackings

Character is forged and convictions best refined in high-pressure spaces. The struggles and disappointments we face as special-needs parents, even our perceptions of "imprisonment," are far humbler than Paul's suffering. Yet we are far more than "just" a mom or dad. We are "just a mom" like God is *just* a Father.

Our children gift us with a unique opportunity for lifelong discipleship. Not every follower of Christ will write a book—much less thirteen. But each of us has our own unique story. God has an individualized spiritual IEP for each of His children. Every believer has the chance to be molded by our unique circumstances. We all have Praetorians who do life with us in our schools, neighborhoods, and communities. They can bear witness to the difference Jesus makes in the "imprisonment" of our pressures and limitations.

Through special-needs parenting, God can deliver us from presumptions on the best way to serve Him. He humbles our grandiose, human plans and overconfidence. He teaches us the secret to being content in any circumstance, regardless of any hijacked hopes. Our child's disability can be the sharpest tool in heaven's drawer to humble, break, and remold our faith and character into greater Christ-likeness.

What feels like oppression can yield new opportunities. What feels like denial of opportunities, God can use to open up new channels for our discipleship. What feels like prison, God can repurpose into a pulpit. What has happened to us will turn out for our deliverance. What has happened to us can serve to advance the gospel.

UNBREAKABLE PROMISES

- "Even though I have received such wonderful revelations from God. So to keep me from becoming proud, I was given a thorn in my flesh, a messenger from Satan to torment me and keep me from becoming proud. Three different times I begged the Lord to take it away. Each time he said, "My grace is all you need. My power works best in weakness." So now I am glad to boast about my weaknesses, so that the power of Christ can work through me. That's why I take pleasure in my weaknesses, and in the insults, hardships, persecutions, and troubles that I suffer for Christ. For when I am weak, then I am strong" (2 Corinthians 12:7–10 NLT).
- "Not only so, but we also glory in our sufferings, because we know that suffering produces perseverance; perseverance, character; and character, hope. And hope does not put us to shame . . ." (Romans 5:3–5).

Prayer

Lord, Your Word promises to keep in perfect peace those whose minds are steadfast, because they trust in You (Isaiah 26:3). No matter what might feel "imprisoning" today—whether internal struggles or external circumstances—help me to trust in Your plans. Show me the secret to being content in any circumstance, believing that what has happened to us, You will repurpose into a blessing for my family, and a testimony to a watching world.

Questions

1. What feels like "imprisonment" or limitations on your life today? Grief, frustrations, or hijacked ambitions? List them out and surrender them before the Lord.
2. What greater work is God accomplishing through these "chains"? What greater gifts might He be cultivating in the confines of your parenting?
3. Who are the Praetorian guards—friends, family, and community—who stand watch from front-row seats to your life? They bear witness to what God is doing in your family. What difference do they see in your countenance?

CHAPTER 22

"What Do We Do Now?"

LOSING OUR WAY ALONG THE WAY

Now that same day two of them were going to a village
called Emmaus . . . As they talked . . . Jesus himself came up
and walked along with them; but they were kept from
recognizing him. He asked them, "What are you discussing . . . ?"
They stood still, their faces downcast. . . . He said to them,
"How foolish you are, and how slow to believe all
that the prophets have spoken! Did not the Messiah have
to suffer these things and then enter his glory?" . . .
As they approached the village . . . Jesus continued on
as if he were going farther. But they urged him strongly,
"Stay with us, for it is nearly evening . . . ." So he went in to stay
with them. Then their eyes were opened and they recognized him,
and he disappeared from their sight. They asked each other,
"Were not our hearts burning within us while he talked
with us on the road and opened the Scriptures to us?"

Luke 24 :13–32

I thought God was supposed to be good! We believed. We followed. We tithed, served, and sacrificed. We even led! After all we've done, how could this happen? I don't know that I can trust Him anymore. What do we do now?"

Perhaps you've never considered God before. Perhaps you recently became a Christian. Or perhaps you've been walking with Christ for years. No matter what your on-ramp to faith or current spiritual address, crisis has a unilateral way of derailing everyone from the intended path. Few things throw us off course more than when our child is diagnosed with a lifelong disability.

Tragedy can upend even the most fervent faith. We lose our way along the way. When all prior convictions, spiritual ambitions, and dreams are lost, then what? How do we reconcile the premise of a "good" God in the face of disappointment and devastation? Bewildered and disoriented, caught between belief and disbelief, we're conflicted and ambivalent about pressing on. How do we keep going? Or do we turn back and abandon our faith? Take comfort. We are not the first walking wounded to face such a crossroad.

A Reckoning En Route

In Luke chapter 24, two disciples stumble along on their journey toward Emmaus. After following hard after Jesus, their hope had died on a cross at Calvary. Convinced Jesus was the Messiah, His followers were devastated at His death. The Savior didn't turn out the way they'd expected. Now, having lost their spiritual bearings, they found themselves downcast and disillusioned. Perplexed at reports of Jesus's empty tomb, they struggled to reconcile the conflict, both within and without.

Amid their confusion, Jesus appeared. Jesus Himself, the very object of their hope and being, came up and walked alongside them. But they failed to recognize Him. Perhaps this was grace by design. He asked them, "What are you discussing together as you walk along?" (v. 17). An omniscient God doesn't ask questions because He lacks understanding or insight. He asks because we do.

Knowing that our faith has stalled, He sidles in close to nudge us along as we wrestle with our doubts. Unbeknownst to us, He presses in close to probe our troubled spirits and coax us into reasoning together. "*What things?*" His glory veiled, He provides us a safe space to voice our doubts and work through them.

When our faith has been crippled and trials sideline our confidence; when we are foolish and slow to believe all that God has promised, the Holy Spirit walks with us to explain what was said in the scriptures concerning Himself (v. 27). Though we may fail to discern His very presence surrounding us, our faulty perceptions have no bearing on God's unassailable character. The Holy Spirit engages with us, interceding when we don't know how to pray (Romans 8:26), guiding and working in our hearts to reaffirm His truth. For it is God who works in us to will and to act in order to fulfill His good purpose (Philippians 2:13).

The Holy Spirit will guide us, to understand deeply what the scriptures say about Him. He desires truth in our inmost parts (Psalm 51:6). Let us sift through the Word and find that His Word sifts through us.

The Road to Recovery

In times of distress and disorientation, our perceptions are often disordered or illogical. We may feel angry toward God and question if He exists; or abandoned by a God we're not sure was ever there. Our confidence has been crushed, leaving us shocked and offended that a "good" God could let our child's disability happen—or continue to happen. Until we reconcile our faith with our reality, we remain shell-shocked, disillusioned, and directionless as we hobble along the road to our Emmaus.

"What now? After all we've gone through, where do we go from here?"

Our internal conflict offers evidence of the Holy Spirit stirring within us. Though our steps may falter, we have not turned back, because deep down, we desire reconciliation with God. Does not our heart burn within us? In such times, we must stay the course. Keep walking and engaging in honest dialogue with God. He grants permission and safe passage to process our doubts with Him.

Seek signs of His presence, believing that angels unaware attend to us. What assumptions or expectations is God parsing out? Allow Him to challenge misconceptions of how He ought to be, how we should be, or what He should do for us. This is how we work out our salvation with fear and trembling. Through our trials, God unearths our shallow understanding and doubts, to mature us into the kind of worshipers the Father seeks.

Seek the mind of Christ. Bid Him to linger and accommodate our questions just awhile longer. The Holy Spirit will sidle up alongside us. He will breathe new life and revelation into His Word, to reveal Himself in increasing measure. We will reacquaint ourselves with the Jesus we thought we'd lost.

As we accept His invitation to reckon and wrestle, we will discover we were never alone. We will conclude that He has been with us—walking, probing, prompting, and blessing—all along. Our road-weary spirits shall be renewed, burning within us with a fresh revelation of who He is.

UNBREAKABLE PROMISES

- "Seek the Lord while he may be found; call upon him while he is near" (Isaiah 55:6).
- "For the eyes of the Lord range throughout the earth to strengthen those whose hearts are fully committed to him" (2 Chronicles 16:9).
- "I pray for you constantly, asking God, the glorious Father of our Lord Jesus Christ, to give you spiritual wisdom and insight so that you might grow in your knowledge of God. I pray that your hearts will be flooded with light so that you can understand the confident hope he has given to those he called—his holy people who are his rich and glorious inheritance" (Ephesians 1:16–18 NLT).
- "Whether you turn to the right or to the left, your ears will hear a voice behind you, saying, 'This is the way; walk in it'" (Isaiah 30:21).

Prayer

Lord, I've lost my way. The confidence I once had in You has been displaced, even disillusioned. But it is exactly then that You draw near, to direct me back to the path of faith. Out of Your grace and mercy, You sidle up closer to strengthen my resolve. Thank You for engaging with my doubts and explaining the scriptures to me again. Please give me a fresh encounter, a new revelation of who You are, that I may resume steadfast steps in pursuit of You.

Questions

1. Where are you in your walk with the Lord? Are you actively seeking, stumbling, or stopped as a result of your child's diagnosis?
2. How is Jesus drawing near and walking alongside you in ways you haven't recognized? What prevents you from recognizing His presence with you?
3. What questions, confusions, or doubts burn in your heart? What truth or clarity is God breathing into your current chaos?

CHAPTER 23

"I Can Never Die"

A SECURE SURRENDER

Near the cross of Jesus stood his mother, his mother's sister,
Mary the wife of Clopas, and Mary Magdalene.
When Jesus saw his mother there, and the disciple
whom he loved standing nearby, he said to her,
"Woman, here is your son," and to the disciple,
"Here is your mother." From that time on,
this disciple took her into his home.
John 19:25–27

I try not to think about my death. Not that I fear death. The Bible assures I am eternally saved through faith in the Son of God, who loved me and gave Himself for me (Galatians 2:20). No. My greatest fear is this: Who will take care of him after I die? Who else on earth could understand, protect, sacrifice, support, or love this complicated bundle like his parents? This is the universal, unspoken fear of every special-needs parent. Our children can't afford to have us die.

Typical parents correctly assume their children will grow up to become independent. Most will. It's a nonissue. Typically developing children will mature and eventually raise families of their own. Some even return to care for their aging parents. Not so for families like ours. Despite his chronological age of sixteen, our son with autism functions at the level of a three-year-old. No doubt, he will continue to make progress over his lifetime. However, in all likelihood, he will remain dependent on others for the rest of his life.

Or for the rest of our lives. Whichever ends first.

Entrusting Unschooled and Ordinary Men

From Jesus's infancy, Simeon had prophesied to Mary, "This child is destined to cause the falling and rising of many in Israel, and to be a sign that will be spoken against, so that the thoughts of many hearts will be revealed. And a sword will pierce your own soul too" (Luke 2:34–35).

As Jesus matured into adulthood, I wonder if He grew increasingly sensitive to the shadow of Calvary drawing near. He knew the day would come when He had to leave His mother behind with a crushed heart and pierced soul. I wonder if He occupied His mind by ministering to the disciples, teaching and feeding the crowds, performing miracles, and challenging the bureaucracy of local religious leaders. I certainly would keep myself distracted to keep from obsessing.

In ancient times, widows and orphans were the most vulnerable of all people, much like orphans, the disabled, and the elderly are in ours. As Mary's firstborn, Jesus would have known He would be responsible for her care. Moments away from His death,

Jesus's last thoughts turned to the dearest, most precious person to Him on earth.

The Son of God had lived a perfect life, fulfilled every prophecy, and submitted to His Father's will. Yet He used His last breaths to ensure His mother would be taken care of. Only then, "knowing that all was now completed . . . he bowed his head and gave up his spirit" (John 19:28, 30 NIV84).

He did not trust humanity because He knew what was in them (John 2:24–25). Yet He who wielded authority to summon legions of angels and supernatural provisions surrendered the care of His dear mother into the hands of a mere mortal, someone "whom he loved, standing nearby" (John 19:26).

Jesus left behind His beloved too. God is well-versed in entrusting His most vulnerable beloved into dubious human hands. The Savior of the world assigned the ministry of reconciliation to "unschooled and ordinary" (Acts 4:13) men. The omnipotent God of the universe entrusted the nurturing of His newborn, fledgling church to a gaggle of human disciples: the very ones who'd completely ditched Him and run, just a few days earlier.

Specifically, He handed the keys to the kingdom to a fumble-prone Simon Peter, named him the rock on whom He would build His church, and vowed that the gates of Hades would not overcome it (Matthew 16:18). Personally, I would have vetted more stringently, selecting from a highly qualified pool of applicants. But God in His sovereignty chose to do it this way.

In 2002, God also dispatched a disabled baby into the care of a woefully underqualified young woman. She scarcely had compassion for the homeless, and tossed around the word *retarded*. God paired this unlikely caregiver with a child who had complex needs.

That woefully underqualified woman was me.

Surrendering Control

In far humbler ways, I, too, am inundated with the daily tasks and responsibilities of feeding, serving, protecting, and advocating. I can avoid having to think about this gnawing, underlying anxiety. But it's always just under the surface.

I'm chronically aware that I have a limited window to serve and advocate for my son. While I am young, healthy, and active, I have the false luxury of avoiding a preoccupation with death. But every once in a while, I'll run into a horrifying article in the news, engage in a candid conversation with a fellow special-needs parent, or a random, trivial incident will trigger a fresh wave of panic, a reflex I must suppress in order to function.

Inevitably, my body will fail. I will start to feel the creaking and groanings of my soul being summoned heavenward. One day, I will have to surrender my beloved into the hands of someone else, perhaps someone blissfully unschooled in autism, and say, "Here is your son" (John 19:26 NLT). I can only pray that I will have someone nearby whom I love, someone I can confidently name and trust to care for my child as their own. God will work through them and supply all their needs in Christ Jesus, just as He had for me when I was his primary caretaker.

In the meantime, I do what I can by way of vitamins, life insurance, special-needs trusts, wills, and conservatorship. But ultimately, I have no idea or control over what will happen to him after I'm gone. Only God knows the future. He who was, and is, and is to come owns the future.

The Lord of the future has compassion for my fears of today. Knowing He understands somehow makes a difference. Knowing that my heavenly Father grieved as I grieve, and surrendered as I must surrender, comforts me greatly. It enables a release and freedom from being obsessed by things over which I have no control. Knowing this kind of compassionate God helps me, quite literally, to rest in peace, in this age and in the age to come.

I don't know many things for certain, who will take care of my son, how he will live, feed, or dress himself, nor the quality or duration of his life. But what I do know are God's promises: "'For I know the plans I have for you,' declares the Lord, 'plans to prosper you and not to harm you, plans to give you hope and a future'" (Jeremiah 29:11).

The Lord knows the plans He has for me, and for my child. Plans to prosper him and not to harm him, plans to give him hope and a future—including the parts that no longer include me.

And the gates of Hades will not overcome it.

UNBREAKABLE PROMISES

- "Cast your cares on the Lord and he will sustain you; he will never let the righteous be shaken" (Psalm 55:22).
- "For I will pour water on the thirsty land, and streams on the dry ground; I will pour out my Spirit on your offspring, and my blessing on your descendants" (Isaiah 44:3).
- "Do not be anxious about anything, but in every situation, by prayer and petition, with thanksgiving, present your requests to God. And the peace of God, which transcends all understanding, will guard your hearts and your minds in Christ Jesus" (Philippians 4:6–7).

Prayer

Lord, You are God and I am not. You love my child even more than I do. You are ultimately responsible for us. Please help me to identify the areas I am responsible for, and surrender unto You the parts only You can control. I want to experience Your peace that transcends understanding, even as I prepare my child for a future someday without me. Please help me to release worry and anxiety, surrender control, and entrust my child to You.

Questions

1. What hinders you from trusting that God has plans to "prosper you and not to harm you, plans to give you hope and a future"? How can you respond to God's invitation to surrender worry about your child's future and experience His peace? What would surrendering control and being at peace look like?
2. How do you distinguish between your responsibility and God's sovereignty? What are the parts only you can do versus what only God can do?
3. What scriptures can you claim in faith for your child's future?

CHAPTER 24

"Why Was He Born This Way?"

CRISIS AND CULPABILITY

As he went along, he saw a man blind from birth. His disciples asked him, "Rabbi, who sinned, this man or his parents, that he was born blind?" "Neither this man nor his parents sinned," said Jesus, "but this happened so that the works of God might be displayed in him."
John 9:1–3

Despite fanatical tracking on pregnancy websites, despite a nine-month ban on raw or unpasteurized foods, despite nightly reading aloud and mild cardiovascular exercise, despite daily pregnancy vitamins and Mozart through headphones resting on my growing belly, we still got autism. We did everything right, didn't we?

When a child is diagnosed with a disability, second-guessing and regrets flood a parent's mind. I thought I'd left no stone unturned in optimal prenatal care. But there was no way to dislodge this mental millstone—only countless ways to sink.

Was it something I ate during pregnancy?

Was it my genes or yours?

Was it something we did, or failed to do?

Is this punishment for secret sin?

We punish ourselves with endless speculation over what we should or shouldn't have done. Everything and everyone becomes suspect, regardless how remote, irrational, and unlikely: defective genes passed on from a distant relative; a contaminated vitamin; poor choices made in younger, wilder days; consequences due to a lack of prayer at best; or closet sin at worst.

Guilt craves something or someone else to blame. It's a brokenness that dates back to the Fall, remapping the emotional DNA of every generation since. Our fallen nature wants to deflect culpability onto anyone else but ourselves.

Is this my fault or is it yours? Was it genetic or environmental? Where did this come from? Who is responsible? Why was our child born this way?

An Enemy Did This

> "Rabbi, who sinned, this man or his parents, that he was born blind?"
>
> —John 9:2

Jesus wasted no time squelching the toxic essence of this question: Who is responsible for this? He replied unequivocally, "Neither this man or his parents sinned" (John 9:3). The Word of God is swift to dispel faulty ideology. Disability is not an act of cosmic justice. There is no karma or condemnation in Christ (Romans 8:1).

Genesis 1 established God's intentions of perfection for His children. He who sows only good seed (Matthew 13:27) would never curse or inflict harm upon His children. In fact, He willingly took the punishment for our sin and nailed it to a cross. A loving and gracious God leans heavily on the side of redemption over retribution.

The Lord doesn't hold the parents responsible for their child's disability. Period. And if He is not the instigator, then who is to blame? We can know, "An enemy did this" (Matthew 13:28). The enemy is an accuser. The father of lies prowls about, seeking to tear down and destroy. His mission has always been to plant seeds of distrust and division between a loving Father and His children.

The enemy finds easy prey in the bleeding hearts of special-needs parents. Satan knows that when disappointment strikes, our instinct is to cry out, "Why? Who is responsible for this?" He exploits and subverts our child's disability to undermine our faith in God's goodness. This enemy continues to deflect responsibility by injecting distrust and suspicion. The same hiss that defamed God's character to Eve, continues to assail the hearts of special-needs parents today, with false accusations, blame, and shame.

If Not Who, Then What?

Regardless of who is responsible for the past, God is responsible for our future. Our responsibility is over the choices and responses we make today. God does not hold us responsible for causing our child's disability. But He does hold us responsible for our response to it.

"Who is responsible for my child's condition?" may easily consume our thoughts. But our Redeemer is already at work to provide a solution. A sovereign and merciful God already knows what He will do (John 6:6). What the enemy intended for harm, God already had in mind to repurpose for good, good, and very good. Remember and trust in God's original intentions. He will do what only a sovereign God can do. He is a redeeming God—the only kind He knows how to be.

Meanwhile, we must do what only we can do for our children. Our responsibility is not fixating on the origins or etiology of our child's disability. Denial, justification, or blame about what happened in the past only squanders our mental energy and steals from the good we can do for our child today.

We know we must surrender the future. Our children cannot afford for us to remain sidelined by factors we had no power to change. We must surrender any voluntary enslavement to dwelling on what happened in the past.

More important than "How did this happen?" is "What will I do now?" Our responsibility is to pivot from obsessing on the past—Whose fault is this?—and focus on our present collaboration with Jesus.

There is much we have to do. Seek the Lord's wisdom to guide our responses, choices, and actions for the many pressing decisions our children need from us today.

There is something even greater that God plans to do. He will prevail over what we could not prevent. Why was our child born this way? Not because we sinned. Not because we failed to merit God's blessing. Not because we're being punished. It was so that the redemptive work of God could be displayed in our child's life.

And in ours.

UNBREAKABLE PROMISES

- "Therefore, there is now no condemnation for those who are in Christ Jesus" (Romans 8:1).
- "There is no fear in love. But perfect love drives out fear, because fear has to do with punishment. The one who fears is not made perfect in love" (1 John 4:18).

- "Now the Lord is the Spirit, and where the Spirit of the Lord is, there is freedom" (2 Corinthians 3:17 ESV).
- "For freedom Christ has set us free; stand firm therefore, and do not submit again to a yoke of slavery" (Galatians 5:1 ESV).
- "The Spirit of the Sovereign LORD is on me, because the LORD has anointed me to proclaim good news to the poor. He has sent me to bind up the brokenhearted, to proclaim freedom for the captives and release from darkness for the prisoners" (Isaiah 61:1).

Prayer

Lord, thank You for Your forgiveness and favor. Your grace clears me from condemnation, and absolves me of guilt. Your Word makes it clear: You don't hold me responsible for my child's disability. An enemy did this. But You will prevail where I could not prevent. Help me not to perseverate on the hows or whys, but to fix my eyes on how You will redeem it. Please reveal what I need to do next, so that the works of God may be displayed through our lives.

Questions

1. In what areas have you been suffering from guilt? What regrets or fears have plagued you regarding your child's disability? What does the Word of God say?
2. What are the next steps you need to take for yourself, for your child, and for your family? Focus on what you need to do now rather than on factors you cannot change.
3. How is the redemptive work of God being displayed through your child's life? How is the grace of God being displayed in yours?

CHAPTER 25

"What Is the Work of God?"

BELIEVING, DESPITE

Jesus answered, "Very truly I tell you, you are looking for me, not because you saw the signs I performed but because you ate the loaves and had your fill. Do not work for food that spoils, but for food that endures to eternal life, which the Son of Man will give you. For on him God the Father has placed his seal of approval." Then they asked him, "What must we do to do the works God requires?" Jesus answered, "The work of God is this: to believe in the one he has sent."

John 6:26–29

"It's a miracle! Their child was cured. God answered their prayers!"

"Have you heard about that new treatment/therapy/vitamin/protocol/special diet? Maybe your child should try it."

"Just pray. Keep praying. God will answer your prayers too."

It's bound to happen. A well-meaning friend, relative, or church member will forward you an inspirational article or video clip.

Perhaps it's a flyer to a church revival or prayer gathering with a famous faith healer, or a testimony, news article, or infomercial extolling a miracle drug, treatment, or diet guaranteed to deliver dramatic results.

Someone got what they prayed for. A blessed soul received deliverance from their suffering. God miraculously delivered them from cancer, disability, or disease, and bundled with it an effusive testimony to the goodness of God.

But what if that someone is never you? God appears to withhold that which we desperately seek. Or He gives us something we never asked for, something we wish He'd take away. Why are some healed but not others? If our child's disability wasn't caused by God but permitted so that God's works might be displayed, where, then, is our miracle?

Believing Despite

In John 6, Jesus had just performed two miracles, back to back. Miraculously feeding thousands of people and walking on water is easy for One who specializes in the impossible. He who wrote the laws of nature maintains authority to bend them. Understandably, the crowds hounded Him, hungry for more spectacular displays of provision and healing. But to these, Jesus countered in verse 27, "Do not work for food that spoils, but for food that endures to eternal life, which the Son of Man will give you."

Jesus frequently curbs our earthly appetites to exhort us to seek food we know nothing about (John 4:32). Because His ways are higher (Isaiah 55:9), the work of God often requires His people to step into realms beyond human reason. Daniel walked into a den of lions, praising God whether He saved him or not; Job trusted in the favor of God, despite forfeiting every earthly evidence of it. Apostle Paul rejoiced in a physical affliction that God never removed.

Countless others in the history of faith never saw their prayers fulfilled. "All these people were still living by faith when they died. They did not receive the things promised; they only saw them and welcomed them from a distance" (Hebrews 11:13). Regardless of outcomes, they believed in God's goodness. This is what the ancients were commended for: maintaining confidence in what they hoped for, and assurance about what they did not see.

While they all prayed for urgent needs, they worshiped God for who He is, apart from what He did—or didn't do—for them. They believed, despite.

Seeking His Face, Not His Hand

The same authority that held sway over the ancients governs over our faith today. It's easy to praise God when He gives us what we want. But what about when He withholds the healing we ask for?

To trust and believe despite not getting what we want runs contrary to our nature. When suffering feels relentless, when others receive spectacular answers to their prayers while ours go unanswered, is it reasonable to expect a rebuffed heart to trust and praise God? "With man it is impossible, but not with God. For all things are possible with God" (Mark 10:27 ESV).

Which is easier, the forgiveness of sins or the healing of a paralyzed body? (Luke 5:23). Which is a greater wonder, a heart that thanks God for healing or one that yet praises Him when He doesn't? He who holds authority over flesh and spirit works miracles in both. It's easy for one who specializes in the impossible.

Dramatic physical healings are indeed miracles of God. Such

demonstrations of power defy logic and science, pointing to the existence of supernatural power. But the work of God also includes the ability to sing, "It is well," when all is not. It includes believing He is good, despite an uncertain future paved by an unknown prognosis. It is the divine ability to rejoice for the answered prayers of others when their children make more progress while our own children continue to lag. It is the inexplicable exchange of resentment and cynicism with defiant hope and joy. The transformation of a bitter heart of stone into a tender heart of flesh is spiritual alchemy only an almighty God can do. Hope in the midst of unanswered prayer is unnatural, unreasonable, and illogical, apart from the supernatural workings of God.

Believing despite is exemplified through the testimony of Joni Eareckson Tada, who remains in a wheelchair after fifty years:

> My affliction has stretched my hope, made me know Christ better, helped me long for truth, led me to repentance of sin, goaded me to give thanks in times of sorrow, increased my faith, and strengthened my character. Being in this wheelchair has meant knowing *Him* better, feeling His pleasure every day. If that doesn't qualify as a miracle in your book, then—may I say in all kindness?—I prefer my book to yours.[22]

Trusting in God does not exempt us from suffering. And suffering does not exempt us from trusting. Jesus Himself is the Bread of Life. The hunger of our souls must be satisfied in who He is, not just the solutions He can provide. Blessed are those who have received healing and fulfillment of their prayers. Even more blessed are those who do not receive, yet believe, despite (John 20:29). When we can seek His face beyond seeking His hand, that is the inexplicable and miraculous work of God displayed.

UNBREAKABLE PROMISES

- "Let us not become weary in doing good, for at the proper time we will reap a harvest if we do not give up. Therefore, as we have opportunity, let us do good to all people, especially to those who belong to the family of believers" (Galatians 6:9–10).
- "Consider it pure joy, my brothers and sisters, whenever you face trials of many kinds, because you know that the testing of your faith produces perseverance. Let perseverance finish its work so that you may be mature and complete, not lacking anything" (James 1:2–4).
- "Therefore, since we are surrounded by such a great cloud of witnesses, let us throw off everything that hinders and the sin that so easily entangles. And let us run with perseverance the race marked out for us, fixing our eyes on Jesus, the pioneer and perfecter of faith. For the joy set before him he endured the cross, scorning its shame, and sat down at the right hand of the throne of God. Consider him who endured such opposition from sinners, so that you will not grow weary and lose heart" (Hebrews 12:1–3).

Prayer

Lord, I want to shift from seeking only Your hand of provision to seeking Your face. Whether You provide what we pray for or You choose to heal in a different matter, I want to know and experience You in a deeper way. Show me how to maintain confidence in the healing I hope for, and assurance about the deliverance I do not yet see. In this way, we demonstrate Your power and glory when we can believe and rejoice in You, despite.

Questions

1. In what other areas can you experience miraculous healing? In what areas can you exercise faith where it's hardest? How might it look to choose hope over despair?
2. How can you go about seeking spiritual food that does not spoil? How can you curb your appetites to prioritize your soul, the spiritual over the physical and material?
3. How is God redefining your definition of *miracle* or *blessing*? Are there other significant miracles God has provided that you may have overlooked due to fixating on dramatic, physical healing? What blessings are *others* experiencing through your child or family? Take a moment to give thanks for these.

CHAPTER 26

"What Do You Want Me to Do for You?"

DUMB QUESTIONS

Then they came to Jericho. As Jesus and his disciples, together with a large crowd, were leaving the city, a blind man, Bartimaeus (which means "son of Timaeus"), was sitting by the roadside begging. When he heard that it was Jesus of Nazareth, he began to shout, "Jesus, Son of David, have mercy on me!" Many rebuked him and told him to be quiet, but he shouted all the more, "Son of David, have mercy on me!" Jesus stopped and said, "Call him." So they called to the blind man, "Cheer up! On your feet! He's calling you." Throwing his cloak aside, he jumped to his feet and came to Jesus. "What do you want me to do for you?" Jesus asked him. The blind man said, "Rabbi, I want to see." "Go," said Jesus, "your faith has healed you." Immediately he received his sight and followed Jesus along the road.

Mark 10:46–52

I heard the unmistakable creak of the snack cabinet door, followed by the guilty crinkle of a chip bag being opened in stealth: all indications of a robbery in progress. I rounded the corner into the kitchen and caught our toddler with a fistful of Doritos, halfway to his mouth. He froze. I froze. After a moment of silent showdown, I finally prompted, "Jeremy, what do you want?"

I knew what he wanted. It was perfectly obvious. But years of speech therapy had trained us to mine for teachable moments like this. I wanted our nonverbal boy with autism to use his words. I wanted him to ask.

"Chip."

"What about chip, Jeremy?"

"I want chip."

"Sure, just one chip? A little or a lot?"

"Lot. Chip. I want lot chip . . ."

"Who are you talking to?"

"Mmmm-ommy. I want lot chip, Mommy."

"Oh! You want a lot of chips? Sure thing, buddy!"

It would have been easier to hand it to him, three minutes ago. But that wasn't the point. We took the time to extract a complete sentence, word by word, however painstaking. It wasn't about the chip. It wasn't about the cheese sticks, Popsicles, or video game. It wasn't even about syntax, diction, or vocabulary.

I just want my child to talk to me. I want him to lean on his parents and find that we delight to help. Someday, I'd love to have an extended conversation, beyond basic needs-driven transactions like these. I want to exchange ideas, to hear his thoughts and heart, and for him to understand ours.

It was about the interaction, the dialogue, and the relationship. As he practices in the safety of home, he can expand to engage with the rest of the world. But we had to start somewhere. That day, it was Mom confiscating a half-eaten bag of chips and asking the obvious, *"Baby, what do you want?"*

It's not for my sake that I ask. It's for his.

Dumb Questions

Throughout the Bible, God appears to ask "dumb" questions of His children, or so it would seem. To a fearful Adam and Eve, "Where are you?" (Genesis 3:9); to a guilt-stricken Cain, "Where is your brother Abel?" (Genesis 4:9); to the desperate woman with the issue of blood, "Who touched my clothes?" (Mark 5:30); to the thirty-eight-year invalid at Bethesda, "Do you want to get well?" (John 5:6); and to a blind Bartimaeus crying out for Him, "What do you want me to do for you?" (Mark 10:51).

An all-knowing God doesn't ask, for lack of knowledge. He already had in mind how He would honor each request. But first, He took a moment to hone in on their deeper issues: to probe and appraise, to dislodge and unearth, to pinpoint and extract the hidden needs they didn't know they had.

For Adam, Eve, and Cain, He provided opportunity for confession and covering for their sins. For the ostracized and bleeding woman, He publicly affirmed her treasured status as a daughter of God. For the invalid, He warned of spiritual diseases and consequences far worse than physical paralysis. And for Bartimeaus, Jesus honored the faith of a blind man who recognized the Messiah, a fact that others with 20/20 vision failed to see.

God sees through to the heart of the matter to accurately diagnose the deepest matters of the heart. Because He prioritizes the condition of our souls, He's a God who forgives our sins *and* heals all our diseases (Psalm 103:3). Our individual diagnoses may differ, but spiritual poverty is a universal condition. The Lord already knows we seek Him as the Great Physician for our children. He also knows we need Him as the healer of the brokenhearted for ourselves.

Help My Unbelief!

God looks beyond the urgent to see the "hidden disabilities" in our hearts. He knows our faith has sustained a hit, perhaps even been crippled by grief. He also appreciates the insufficiency of pat or clichéd answers. His instrument for probing can come in the form of an awkward question, posed with noble intent. Jesus's aim is not to merely dress a wound but heal it from within. He desires truth in our innermost parts. God already has in mind what He's going to do for our children. But first, He may tarry for our sakes, to help our unbelief (Mark 9:24). He's willing to risk being misunderstood so that we may know and be known, helped, and healed.

What do we want Jesus to do for us? Obviously, we want our children to be healthy and whole. Their needs and well-being legitimately occupy the bulk of our prayers. As parents, we've experienced firsthand the frustration of being dismissed, unable to secure an accurate diagnosis or treatment. Our child's disability is not our only pressing need. We each have our own internal impairments that go long untreated too. Our children may require urgent care. But our souls need critical care as well.

Put Your Mask on First

Flight attendants announce at the beginning of every takeoff, "Parents, put your oxygen mask on first. Then assist any small children."

We offer no benefit to our children when we are depleted of breath, strength, or hope. Our families depend on us for physical care, but also to impart courage, strength, vitality, and hope. We cannot give what we do not have. Time is legitimately scarce in the daily rigors of special-needs caregiving. It's easy to relegate ourselves as secondary to our children's more pressing needs. Our children have particular needs. But we do, too. Because our children's well-being depends on our own, we cannot afford to neglect our physical or spiritual health. We cannot serve them well, with our utmost capacity, if we are chronically shriveled in mind, body, or spirit.

What do we really need for Him to do for us? Our Father knows we grow weary. He understands the burden of carrying a responsibility no one else can understand. Jesus will pause to lay hold of teachable moments. He bids us come to a solitary place, to rest with Him for a while (Mark 6:31), to refresh, restore, and rehabilitate our faltering faith.

Our heavenly Father will gently probe and prompt us to confess unexpressed needs, struggles, and frustrations. He does not leave us to forage on our own. He desires to engage with His children in intimate dialogue, to hear our hearts and have us know His. Let us use whatever halting words we have to confess, "Lord, I want __________. I want to see You. Please help my unbelief!" It's not about the diagnosis or disability. It's not about the doubts or despair. Ultimately, it's about the relationship Jesus wants to repair and restore with His children: for us to lean on Him and discover that He delights to help, heal, and give hope.

"Do you want to get well?" (John 5:6). "What do you want me to do for you?" (Mark 10:51). It's not for His sake—or even our child's—that He asks. It's for ours.

UNBREAKABLE PROMISES

- "Without faith it is impossible to please God, because anyone who comes to him must believe that he exists and that he rewards those who earnestly seek him" (Hebrews 11:6).
- "'If you can'?" said Jesus. "'Everything is possible for one who believes.'" Immediately the boy's father exclaimed, "'I do believe; help me overcome my unbelief!'" (Mark 9:23–24).
- "Take delight in the LORD, and he will give you the desires of your heart" (Psalm 37:4).
- "But seek first his kingdom and his righteousness, and all these things will be given to you as well. Therefore do not worry about tomorrow, for tomorrow will worry about itself. Each day has enough trouble of its own" (Matthew 6:33–34).

Prayer

Lord, I want to see. I want to see healing for my child. You already know what I desperately want for You to do for us. But You want me to ask, to engage with You in prayer. I also want to see You, and come to a greater conviction of who You are, and Your power at work within us. Help me overcome my unbelief!

Questions

1. What do you want Jesus to do for you? Do *you* want to get well, not just your child to be healed? Are you equally urgent for your own spiritual healing and strength? God already knows what we seek. But He delights to hear from us, however halting or awkward our prayers may be.

2. What awkward question is Jesus asking you? What deeper need or hidden disability of the heart is He probing and prompting you to address?
3. How is prayer and conversation with God deepening your dependence on Him?

CHAPTER 27

"What Good Could Come from This?"

LOW EXPECTATIONS

Philip found Nathanael and told him,
"We have found the one Moses wrote about in the Law,
and about whom the prophets also wrote—
Jesus of Nazareth, the son of Joseph."
"Nazareth! Can anything good come from there?"
Nathanael asked. "Come and see," said Philip.
John 1:45–46

For years, the Tooth Fairy came for Jeremy's younger brother, Justin, but she never came for Jeremy. She had dismissed the possibility that a nonverbal child could understand such abstract notions. What good would it do, other than confuse the poor child? The all-knowing Tooth Fairy must have relayed the memo to Santa, because every December 25, he, too, bypassed our home.

One evening, Jeremy tugged me urgently toward my desk. *"Ah-va-lope. Ah-va-lope!"* He wanted an envelope? How did he even know the word? It wasn't on his IEP vocabulary list. Curious, I handed him one. He fished a tooth from his pocket and placed it into the envelope. Evidently, he'd pulled the tooth on his own. He scampered to his room and slipped the envelope under his pillow. Giggling and pleased with himself, he nestled in to wait for sleep.

My heart shattered into a million pieces of regret. For over a decade, I had lowballed my expectations. I wrongly assumed Jeremy couldn't understand. But why wouldn't he? For years, he had witnessed his younger brother exchange tooth after tooth, and watched it transform into dollar bills in the morning. It didn't matter if it was the Tooth Fairy, osmosis, or black magic. He didn't need to understand to enjoy its benefits. He just knew that it worked: a tooth inserted under a pillow would convert to cash by morning. Of course Jeremy would want the same.

My unbelief had cheated him years of joy. Now, he took matters into his own hands. Wracked with guilt and remorse, I lamented and wished for a million dollars to compensate for the years of giggles we'd forfeited. I vowed to never underestimate him again.

Can Anything Good Come from This?

"Nazareth! Can anything good come from there?"
—John 1:46

The small town of Nazareth was easy to dismiss. A remote agricultural village, it barely registered a blip on the ancient map. There, the son of a humble carpenter grew up in obscurity. Like a root out of dry ground, "he had no beauty or majesty to attract us to him;

nothing in his appearance that we should desire him" (Isaiah 53:2). No one expected anything good to come from there.

He flew under the radar for decades. Upon His commencement into public ministry, His claims as the Son of God were dismissed as the ravings of a madman, a lunatic, or a liar. No one could conceive Him as Lord. Even the few who sought Him out harbored their doubts. From Jairus's dying daughter to the incurably bleeding woman, their predicaments were too far gone. Their pleas came too late. "Why bother the teacher anymore?" (Mark 5:35). What good would it do?

At the Nazarene's death, the skies went dark and the earth trembled to concur in resignation: it was finished. The end. The self-proclaimed Messiah entered the world amidst the filth of animals, only to endure a death more ignoble than His birth. Days later, His followers convened to prepare His body (Mark 16:1–7). Despondent and hopeless, they all wondered, *What now? What good could come from this?*

Bleak landscapes have been the birthplaces of life before. The Bible opens with the Spirit of God hovering over the formless and empty, perfectly positioned to usher in light, order, and fruitfulness. A rapid succession of good, good, and very good stood ready in the wings, awaiting their grand entrance into the darkest deep. Even when that creation fell, irrepressible grace instantly invoked a disaster recovery plan. It persisted through generations of human waywardness, and finally, overturned death and despair into the best, worst Good Friday in history.

Some endings don't end in death. Some beginnings are birthed only after a kernel of wheat falls to the ground and dies (John 12:24). So it is with the death of a dream.

Resetting the Bar, Higher

"Your child may never learn to walk, talk, or live independently."
"She'll need lifelong support and treatment."
"Life expectancy is usually only _______."

A doctor's worst-case scenarios only underscore the dread already in a special-needs parent's heart: our child may never go to college, enjoy a career, marry, or raise a family. The list of "may nevers" is endless and cruel.

"Some trust in chariots and some in horses, but we trust in the name of the Lord our God" (Psalm 20:7). Some may strive for best-case prognoses. Others resign themselves to worst-case scenarios. I made the regrettable mistake of expecting too little of our son, but he schools me time and time again. To my shame, my child's faith in a fairy tale proved stronger than my faith in the Lord.

Jeremy didn't need to understand the mechanics of the Tooth Fairy to enjoy her magic. He believed because he had seen it work in the past. Proof delivered itself under his brother's pillow every time. Past consistency was a reliable predictor of her future performance. What he'd witnessed thus far was enough for him to bank on. He trusted that she would come through again.

This child, with his limited understanding, grasped on to a truth that his mother completely missed. God's faithfulness in the past is a reliable predictor of His trustworthiness in the future. "If we are faithless, he remains faithful, for he cannot disown himself" (2 Timothy 2:13).

> Therefore if you have any encouragement from being united with Christ, if any comfort from his love, if any common sharing in the Spirit, if any tenderness and compassion, then

> make my joy complete by being like-minded, having the same love, being one in spirit and of one mind (Philippians 2:1–2).

Have we experienced encouragement from being united with Christ in the past? If we can recall past testimonies of His comfort, compassion, reassurance, and grace, then we have witnessed enough of God's character to bank on. We can trust that He will come through again.

To our detriment, we lowball the miracles God can do. We won't let ourselves imagine for fear of our hopes getting crushed again. But we don't need to understand how miracles work in order to enjoy them. God will bless our children and exceed our expectations. Could anything good come from our child's disability? No one expected anything good to come from Nazareth either. Let us not subject our own children to "the soft bigotry of low expectations."[23] We cannot afford to underestimate what God can do for our children and through them.

God continues to esteem His children as fearfully and wonderfully made. His works are wonderful. We know that full well (Psalm 139:14). Let God reset the bar of what is possible. Continue to expect great things from a great God, for that is the only kind He knows how to be. According to our faith, it will be done for us (Matthew 9:28–30). What good could come from our child's disability? We need only "Come and see . . ."

UNBREAKABLE PROMISES

- "Now we did not receive the spirit of the world, but we received the Spirit that is from God so that we can know all that God has given us" (1 Corinthians 2:12 NCV).

- "Wait for and confidently expect the LORD; be strong and let your heart take courage; yes, wait for and confidently expect the LORD" (Psalm 27:14 AMP).
- "The LORD will accomplish what concerns me; Your loving kindness, O LORD, is everlasting; do not forsake the works of Your hands" (Psalm 138:8 NASB).
- "God chose the foolish things of the world to shame the wise. God chose the weak things of the world to shame the strong" (1 Corinthians 1:27 NIRV).
- "No eye has seen, no ear has heard, and no mind has imagined what God has prepared for those who love him" (1 Corinthians 2:9–10 NLT).

Prayer

Lord, I confess that since the diagnosis I've harbored low expectations for my child and for our lives. I surrender these worldly ways of valuing and esteeming, in exchange for hope and confidence in what You alone can do. Renew my mind to see as You see. For nothing is impossible with God. Surprise us, Lord. Overwhelm us with unexpected, exceeding, and unsurpassed miracles. I don't need to understand Your miracles to experience them.

Questions

1. Name a past situation you dismissed as hopeless that God transformed into an unexpected blessing. How has a death or loss ended up being life-giving instead? List the ways God has used past pains to birth present blessings. Let these remind you of His faithfulness over today and tomorrow.

2. What expectations have you dismissed as hopeless? What do you struggle to surrender? Are there prayers you've given up on because you feel God is unresponsive, or because you've lost hope?
3. What is God asking you to do today, despite your skepticism, despair, or resignation? Is there an "envelope" you need to submit in faith? *"What good could come from this?"* Despite the pain of loss, what new thing might God be ushering in?

CHAPTER 28

"How Can My Child Live a Worthy Life?"

KINGDOM CURRENCY

So from now on we regard no one from a worldly point of view. Though we once regarded Christ in this way, we do so no longer.

2 Corinthians 5:16

"*He won't have friends.*"

"*He can't go to college.*"

"*He won't be able to work or have a career.*"

"*He won't get married or have a family.*"

"*He won't be independent. He'll need others to always take care of him.*"

The slippery slope from the confirmation of diagnosis to the dissolution of dreams is steep and cruel. Regardless of how rare a child's diagnosis, every special-needs parent's mind slips into a universal pit of despair, as if bound to an unalterable script.

"What will our child's life amount to?"

"What will become of him?"

"Who will love and take care of him?"

"How can He know God?"

But God's ways are higher than ours. What if the earthly trappings we fear as losses for our children are, as Apostle Paul concluded, actually worthless when compared with the infinite value of knowing Christ Jesus our Lord (Philippians 3:8)?

A Successful Life

More than two thousand years ago, a newborn baby spent His first hours in a trough, surrounded by livestock rather than stuffed animals. Relegated to a stable for a makeshift nursery, His parents' social standing had been too humble for better treatment. He grew up in a remote, dusty town as the adopted son of a man who built furniture for a living. He demonstrated insight and made declarations remarkable for a young boy (Luke 2:42–51). His temperament suggested an otherworldly nature; perhaps His neighbors and own family members thought Him peculiar. They'd never encountered anyone quite like Him.

There was nothing particularly attractive about His appearance. He grew up misunderstood and underappreciated, a trend that worsened severely as He got older and resulted in extreme bullying. He never went to college or owned His own home; never married or raised His own children.

In every metric of adult achievement and worldly success, He "failed." This was God's beloved Son, with whom He was well pleased. The heavens opened to celebrate His arrival—the closest He ever came to a commencement ceremony—yet our world esteemed Him not.

> Jesus had no servants, yet they called Him Master. Had no degree, yet they called Him Teacher. Had no medicines, yet they called Him Healer. He had no army, yet kings feared Him. He won no military battles, yet He conquered the world. He committed no crime, yet they crucified Him. He was buried in a tomb, yet He lives today.[24]

He accomplished all this without a degree, career, marriage, family, or the loyalty of friends. No one else ascended to heaven and sits at the right hand of God. No one else achieved eternal glory despite a deficiency of earthly credentials. No one else has been a Savior.

Disabled, Not Discounted

Our world makes clear what it considers signs of success. The idols of our day are wealth, power, fame, beauty, education, elite social standing, or an impressive job title. But in God's economy, favor, blessing, success, and achievement are defined in currency that runs countercultural to our world.

But what is the greatest commandment? "'Love the Lord your God with all your heart and with all your soul and with all your mind.' This is the first and greatest commandment. And the second is like it: 'Love your neighbor as yourself'" (Matthew 22:37–39).

What is God's minimal standard or expectation for His children? "The Lord has told you, human, what is good; he has told you what he wants from you: to do what is right to other people, love being kind to others, and live humbly, obeying your God (Micah 6:8 NCV).

In this way, Jesus lived a life of unparalleled success. He loved the Lord with all His heart, soul, and mind, and loved His neighbor as Himself. He lived incomparably rich in justice, righteousness, mercy, humility—knowing and being known by God. Jesus had no other ambition but to avail Himself to His Father's purposes.

"Weaker," Indispensable Parts

Our children, too, can love the Lord with all their heart, soul, and mind—and love their neighbors as they love themselves. They can seek righteousness, love mercy, and walk humbly before our God. They can know God and be known by Him. Beloved children need not prove their utilitarian value to establish their worth. Whether a man owns a bank or robs one, his mother will cherish him with an inviolable love. Children are valuable because they are loved.

We are loved because we are God's children. While we were yet sinners, Christ died for us (Romans 5:8). He loved us when we were most unworthy, for no other reason than because we are His. Likewise, before our children accomplish any worldly success, we value and adore them for no other reason than because they are ours. The devotion we have for our children is a manifestation of His unconditional love.

What will our child's life amount to? What will become of him? Who will love and take care of him? How can he know God? God can also use our children as a vehicle of blessing. Every child of God—regardless of intake, output, or ability—is equally priceless and purposed by God. His power made perfect in weakness. They offer gifts of the purest love and affection; they humble and heal us from our natural bent toward shallowness, self-sufficiency, and selfishness; and they drive us to our knees in prayer. Our children keep us bowed near the cross, a dreaded posture our flesh would ordinarily avoid. For the follower of Christ, desperate dependence on the Lord is the best place to be. Through our striving to maximize our child's potential, God is working to maximize ours.

There is a reason why God declares "parts of the body that seem weakest and least important are actually the most necessary" (1 Corinthians 12:22 NLT). He bestows greater honor to the parts of the body who lack it. The people who embrace our fallen world may appraise each other by their output and merit. According to their standards, they may view our children as lesser. But "from now on we regard no one from a worldly point of view. Though we once regarded Christ in this way, we do so no longer" (2 Corinthians 5:16).

UNBREAKABLE PROMISES

- "Every good and perfect gift is from above, coming down from the Father of the heavenly lights, who does not change like shifting shadows" (James 1:17).
- "Do not conform to the pattern of this world, but be transformed by the renewing of your mind. Then you will be able to test and approve what God's will is—his good, pleasing and perfect will" (Romans 12:2).
- "Trust in the LORD with all your heart, and lean not on your own understanding" (Proverbs 3:5).
- "We demolish arguments and every pretension that sets itself up against the knowledge of God, and we take captive every thought to make it obedient to Christ" (2 Corinthians 10:5).
- "I could have no greater joy than to hear that my children are following the truth" (3 John 1:4 NLT).

Prayer

Father, forgive me for viewing disability as being "broken" or lesser. That is how the world sees, but not as You do. You esteem my child as wonderfully and fearfully made. Please renew my perspective to have the mind of Christ. You accomplished eternal glory without any of the worldly trappings I fear my child will go without. Bless us in kingdom currency, our value measured in the blood of Christ. May we submit to Your countercultural ways in humility and surrender, so that our lives may reflect Your glory and grace.

Questions

1. How does the "normal" world define success or markers of a valuable life? In contrast, how does God's Word define blessing, success, or a life well lived?
2. How have your values and perspectives been challenged or changed as a result of your child's disability?
3. What is your greatest wish or prayer for your child's life, for your family, and for yourself?

CHAPTER 29

How Is This "Blessed and Highly Favored"?

INCONCEIVABLY MORE

In the sixth month of Elizabeth's pregnancy, God sent the angel Gabriel to Nazareth, a town in Galilee, to a virgin pledged to be married to a man named Joseph, a descendant of David. The virgin's name was Mary. The angel went to her and said, "Greetings, you who are highly favored! The Lord is with you." Mary was greatly troubled at his words and wondered what kind of greeting this might be. But the angel said to her, "Do not be afraid, Mary; you have found favor with God. You will conceive and give birth to a son, and you are to call him Jesus. He will be great and will be called the Son of the Most High. The Lord God will give him the throne of his father David, and he will reign over Jacob's descendants forever; his kingdom will never end." "How will this be," Mary asked the angel, "since I am a virgin?" The angel answered, "The Holy Spirit will come on you, and the power of the Most High will overshadow you. So the holy one to be born will be called the Son of God. Even Elizabeth your relative is going to have a child in her old age, and she who was said to be unable to conceive is in her sixth month. For no word from God will ever fail." "I am the Lord's servant," Mary answered. "May your word to me be fulfilled." Then the angel left her.

Luke 1:26–38

Autism. The moment our pediatric neurologist confirmed our worst fears, every Hallmark-card notion I'd entertained about motherhood evaporated in a nanosecond: baseball games and birthday parties, graduations and mother-son wedding dances. These were the joys every parent assumes as a birthright. But they were gone, wiped away and replaced by five digits of a diagnostic code, 299.00.

The unceasing hemorrhaging of money we didn't have for mounting medical expenses, a gnawing sense of incompetence, and crushing, bone-weary fatigue. For twenty-four hours a day, seven days a week, three hundred sixty-five days, for a lifetime of years, *"There is no known cure."*

While other parents eagerly anticipated their child's future, we looked to ours with dread. Other families looked forward to a world of unlimited possibilities; ours had been shut down by unexpected closures and restrictions. We had to prepare for our deaths when our child was only aged two. *What then will become of him? Who will take care of him when we're gone?*

"Special-needs children are a blessing!" they told me. With both fists raised to the skies, I protested violently. How dare anyone call this "blessed and highly favored"! I could do without such favors. How were we to handle all this? How will this be? Evidently, God defined "blessing" far differently than I did.

"Blessed and Highly Favored"?

Betrothed to an honorable Jewish carpenter, young Mary had a respectable life to look forward to. Until an angel of the Lord appeared and upended her orderly plans. "Greetings, you who are highly favored! The Lord is with you" (v. 28). "Do not be afraid, Mary; you have found favor with God. You will conceive and give birth to a son, and you are to call him Jesus" (vv. 30–31).

How could this be? It sounded impossible. It *was* impossible. The angel was wise to begin with "Do not be afraid!" Who wouldn't be terrified, accosted by a celestial being bearing such news? Surely, such a proclamation felt like no favor at all. Mary was justifiably shocked and fearful, especially when the blessing included, "This child is destined to cause the falling and rising of many in Israel, and to be a sign that will be spoken against, so that the thoughts of many hearts will be revealed. And a sword will pierce your own soul too" (Luke 2:34–35).

Jesus's life was to bring wondrous joy; but His suffering and death, incomparable agony. As the mother of the suffering Savior, a man of sorrows and acquainted with grief (Isaiah 53:3), Mary, too, would suffer. The most blessed among women (Luke 1:42) would endure the worst pain a mother could face: the torture and death of her own child. From the cradle to an early grave, Mary's parenting journey was destined to be a complicated bundle. There was no anesthetizing the truth: some extraordinary blessings are birthed conjoined with pain.

Inconceivable Realities

Like Mary, motherhood hadn't panned out the way I expected. Unlike Mary, I didn't respond in gracious surrender. On August 20, 2004, when we received our child's diagnosis, I couldn't have imagined the journey that lay ahead of us. Lifelong disability felt like a curse. Consumed with grief, it was inconceivable how disability could ever be a blessing. But reflecting on over a decade of grace, our lives have indeed been blessed, immeasurably more than we could have asked or imagined.

I couldn't have imagined the gifted professionals we'd meet along the journey: therapists, educators, clinicians, and specialists who taught, stretched, challenged, and blessed our child in innumerable ways we are forever indebted to. They championed for him with a passion and dedication that paralleled our own. They became a fellow army of trusted allies, advisors, confidants, and counselors.

I couldn't have imagined the selfless leaders and volunteers of special-needs ministries who'd overwhelm us with love, respite, support, and encouragement. As parents, we were drafted into the world of disability; we had a biological obligation to help our child. But volunteers with no obligation to our family, but by the blood of Christ, enlisted to serve and to bless.

I couldn't have imagined the inspiring tribe of fellow special-needs families we'd meet, who have become cherished friends and extended family we chose for ourselves. We understood each other, in a world where no one else does. We offer each other the rare and priceless gift of normalcy and belonging.

I couldn't have imagined how He would use our child to inspire and change others. Disability breathes into life the truth imbedded in 1 Corinthians 12: the parts of the body of Christ considered "weakest" are the most needed. Special-needs families give the church an opportunity to flex its compassion muscles and demonstrate that we are His disciples by how we love one another (John 13:35) in countercultural, extravagant ways.

Most of all, I couldn't have imagined how disability would deliver me from a "country club" type of Christianity. It shattered my armchair religion and galvanized it into an unbreakable faith. God used disability to break and remold me, to make level paths so that my feeble faith could be healed (Hebrews 12:13).

Mary couldn't have possibly conceived. Yet she did. I couldn't have conceived being blessed by disability. Yet I was. *God* redeemed and repurposed our pain, for nothing is impossible with God (Luke 1:37).

Inconceivable Promises, Undeniable Realities

> Faith is deliberate confidence in the character of God whose ways we may not understand at the time.
> —Oswald Chambers[25]

A sword may pierce our souls today. Perhaps the fresh wounds of a diagnosis, or the phantom pangs of grief that strike long afterward. Our child with a disability may not be the one we expected—or the idealized child we wanted. But God will repurpose disability, to refashion us into warriors and witnesses we didn't know we could be.

As impossible as it may sound, we can consider ourselves "blessed and highly favored." Like with Mary, God will heal and fill our deepest disappointments with incomparable blessing. He will accomplish it in a way only a mysterious and unfathomable God can. Mary couldn't have conceived the wondrous realities of Jesus, yet she did. We cannot conceive how disability can be a blessing, yet it shall be.

In the meantime, stow away His promises as we wait for their fulfillment. Like Mary, treasure up all these things and ponder them in our hearts. Let us avail ourselves of God's mysterious and inconceivable ways. May our profession be "Let it be to me as You have said." As we submit to God's will for how He wants to work in our lives, His Spirit will overshadow our grief, fear, and doubt.

Leave room for wonder and hope for the future. Consider that God defines blessing differently than in our economy. May His Word to us be fulfilled. "Blessed is she who has believed that the Lord would fulfill his promises to her!" (Luke 1:45).

UNBREAKABLE PROMISES

- "Ask me and I will tell you remarkable secrets you do not know about things to come" (Jeremiah 33:3 NLT).
- "No eye has seen, no ear has heard, and no mind has imagined what God has prepared for those who love him" (1 Corinthians 2:9 NLT).
- "For nothing will be impossible with God" (Luke 1:37 NASB).
- "Blessed is she who has believed that the Lord would fulfill his promises to her!" (Luke 1:45).
- "Now set your mind and heart to seek the LORD your God" (1 Chronicles 22:19 ESV).
- "Now to him who is able to do immeasurably more than all we ask or imagine, according to his power that is at work within us, to him be glory in the church and in Christ Jesus throughout all generations, forever and ever! Amen" (Ephesians 3:20–21).

Prayer

Lord, how will this be? How can disability possibly be a blessing? What is inconceivable and impossible in the flesh is possible in You. We claim your promises in advance, trusting You for glorious things to come for our children and families. May it be to us as You have said.

Questions

1. Today, what "pierces your soul" with terror, hope, pain, and wonder?
2. Identify a scripture to claim in advance, "to treasure and ponder" in your heart in the meantime.

3. In what ways have you have been surprisingly "blessed and highly favored" in your special-needs parenting journey? How has God worked "for your good" (Romans 8:28), even now?

AUTHOR'S NOTE

In 2004, when our eldest son was diagnosed with autism, all urgent intervention focused on his needs. Rightly so. But his mother had been "crippled," too, both emotionally and spiritually. Christian parents often feel unable to acknowledge their anger and disillusionment under the misconception that faith leaves no room for earnest struggle. Regardless of how rare a diagnosis, and irrespective of family background, genetics, or socioeconomics, every special- needs parent struggles with a universal dilemma: how to reconcile the premise of a good God with the disappointing realities of raising a child with lifelong disability.

How could God let this happen to my child? Does He care? Is He good or even real? How is the Bible relevant to all this? How dare anyone call this a "blessing." Will God heal? In response to the deliverance I desperately sought, God healed the hidden disabilities of my own heart: He restored my broken faith. What the enemy intended for harm, God redeemed for our good. What I thought would destroy us actually galvanized and transformed our faith. Ultimately, our child's disability drove us closer to the heart of God.

In time, the Lord repurposed our struggles into a desire to comfort others with the comfort received from Christ (2 Corinthians 1:4). *Unbroken Faith* was born after years of wrestling with God's promises. It zeroes in on the unseen wounds that fester deep in a special-needs parent's heart. It gives voice to the squelched doubts, questions, grief, and anguish we are afraid to express, and examines them under the Great Physician's revealing light.

For parents of a child with special needs, I pray you find comfort and hope in the God who draws near. He understands, mourns, and grieves with us like no other. God will heal His children. He is more than able. Whether He chooses to heal our children on this side of heaven is His responsibility. How we respond is ours. He is God, and we are not. In the meantime, He is dealing with our spiritual disability. He is working mighty miracles of healing and restoration in *us*.

At the same time, the enemy seeks to exploit our child's disability to maim and disable our faith. He seeks to convince us that our children are broken, and that God cannot be trusted. The enemy lies. No weapon formed against us shall prevail. I pray you find spiritual recovery and newfound resilience; that our "light and momentary troubles are achieving for us an eternal glory that far outweighs them all" (2 Corinthians 4:17): the rousing rebirth of an unbreakable faith.

For friends, family, and support community surrounding a family affected by disability, I pray you find insight and understanding for the unspoken cries of a special-needs family. Thank you for being our first responders. Just as our children may rely on their parents for the rest of their lives, we, too, need your compassion and support, more than words could ever express.

Our God is a redeeming God, the only kind He knows how to be. He cannot help but do immeasurably more than we could ask or imagine.

See, I am doing a new thing! Now it springs up; do you not perceive it? I am making a way in the wilderness and streams in the wasteland.
—Isaiah 43:19

Wrecked, redeemed, and repurposed,
Diane

EPILOGUE

On August 20, 2004, a single piece of paper wrecked and gutted my family. At the time, we despised hearing, "Special-needs children are a blessing!" More than a decade later, we now glorify and praise God for all the things we have heard and seen, which were just as we had been told (Luke 2:20).

Since then, our family has been struck with additional diagnoses and a variety of other devastations. To date, the "thorn" of special-needs parenting still hasn't been removed. Our son hasn't been fully healed of his hidden disabilities or impairments. The rest of the family hasn't either.

Jeremy is now sixteen years old. Mostly nonverbal, he functions socially at the level of a three- or four-year-old. Prone to wandering, he requires constant supervision. In particular, he commands an audience for his nightly "singing" performances (echolalia) at four o'clock every morning. We anticipate these concerts to run indefinitely, and have booked accordingly by way of special-needs conservatorship and such.

He still giggles out loud at inside jokes that appear exclusive to him, God, and the angels. We look forward to getting in on the joke once we install our resurrection ears in heaven. In the meantime, his hilarity is contagious. The world can't help but join in.

Jeremy has triggered the launch of special-needs ministries at several local churches, and counting. He has inspired the careers of teachers, special-education professionals, and autism specialists: friends, family, church community, and volunteers forever changed by a nonverbal boy who never uttered a word of career advice.

As an undercover urban missionary, he continues to serve as a living, breathing—and giggling—show-and-tell of timeless Biblical truths. "God chose the foolish things of the world to shame the wise; God chose the weak things of the world to shame the strong" (1 Corinthians 1:27).

"What has happened to me" (Philippians 1:12) in 2004, and every trial since, has resulted in *Unbroken Faith*. Published more than a decade after our diagnosis D-day, I couldn't have imagined that my raw and impassioned, late-night ravings—private journals compiled into my own book of psalms—would one day be repurposed and redeployed in service of others. The Author and Perfecter of our faith had every chapter mapped out, long before I ever did.

Our son has been the sharpest tool in heaven's drawer to chisel and transform his parents, brother, extended family, and community. One of his greatest contributions has been extracting the best out of everyone around him. In this way, he proves "those parts of the body that seem to be weaker are indispensable" (1 Corinthians 12:22). We are the disciples, parents, leaders, advocates, and influencers we are today because of who our child is, how God has blessed him and made him a blessing. We are not healed, but we have conquered disability. *Conquer* doesn't mean bypass, mitigate, or alleviate. It means conquer. In all these things, we are more than conquerors through Him who loved us (Romans 8:37). Because of Christ, our faith, character, and convictions have made us strong in once broken places.

Additional Resources

PARENT SUPPORT

Kelly Langston, *Autism's Hidden Blessings: Discovering God's Promises for Autistic Children and Their Families.* (Kregel, 2009).

Beyond Suffering Bible NLT: Where Struggles Seem Endless, God's Hope Is Infinite.(Tyndale House Publishers, 2016).

Jolene Philo, *The Caregiver's Notebook: An Organizational Tool and Support to Help You Care for Others.* (Discovery House, 2014).

Emily Colson, *Dancing With Max: A Mother and Son Who Broke Free.* (Zondervan, 2010).

Jolene Philo, *A Different Dream for My Child: Meditations for Parents of Critically or Chronically Ill Children.* (Discovery House, 2011).

Jolene Philo, *Different Dream Parenting: A Practical Guide to Raising a Child with Special Needs.* (Discovery House, 2011).

Doug Mazza and Steve Bundy, *A Different Kind of Courage: God's Design for Fathers of Families Affected by Disability.* (Joni and Friends, 2014).

Kelli Ra Anderson, *Divine Duct Tape: A Devotional Journey in Luke.* (Fox Burrow Media, 2011).

Laurie Wallin, *Get Your Joy Back: Banishing Resentment and Reclaiming Confidence in Your Special Needs Family.* (Kregel Publications, 2015).

Amy Julia Becker, *A Good and Perfect Gift: Faith, Expectations, and a Little Girl Named Penny*. (Bethany House, 2011).

Sandra Peoples and Lee Peoples, Jr., *Held: Learning to Live in God's Grip: A Bible Study for Special Needs Parents.* (CreateSpace, 2013).

Ken Tada and Joni Eareckson Tada, *Joni and Ken: An Untold Love Story*. (Zondervan, 2015).

Andrew and Rachel Wilson, *The Life We Never Expected: Hopeful Reflections on the Challenges of Parenting Children with Special Needs.* (Crossway, 2016).

Nancy Guthrie, *Holding On to Hope: A Pathway through Suffering to the Heart of God.* (Tyndale Momentum, 2006).

Nancy Guthrie, *The One Year Book of Hope.* (Tyndale Momentum, 2005).

Kathi Lipp and Cheri Gregory, *Overwhelmed: How to Quiet the Chaos and Restore Your Sanity.* (Harvest House, 2017).

Joni Eareckson Tada, *A Place of Healing: Wrestling with the Mysteries of Suffering, Pain, and God's Sovereignty.* (David C. Cook, 2015).

Lorna Bradley, *Special Needs Parenting: From Coping to Thriving.* (Huff Publishing Associates, 2015).

Cindy and Joe Ferrini, *Unexpected Journey: When Special Needs Change Our Course.* (Morris Publishing, 2009).

Timothy Keller, *Walking with God through Pain and Suffering.* (Penguin Books, 2015).

Joni Eareckson Tada and Steve Estes, *When God Weeps: Why our Sufferings Matter to the Almighty.* (Zondervan, 2000).

Not Alone (blog) http://specialneedsparenting.net/

Special Needs Ministry Print Resources

Barbara J. Newman, *Autism and Your Church: Nurturing the Spiritual Growth of People with Autism Spectrum Disorder.* (Faith Alive Christian Resources, 2011).

Debbie Lillo and Sib Charles, *Doing Life Together: Building Community for Families Affected by Disability (The Irresistible Church Series).* (Joni and Friends, 2017).

Jolene Philo and Katie Wetherbee, *Every Child Welcome: A Menu of Strategies for Including Kids with Special Needs.*

Amy Fenton Lee, *Leading a Special Needs Ministry: A Practical Guide to Including Children and Loving Families.* (B&H Publishing Group, 2016).

Stephanie Hubach, *Same Lake, Different Boat: Coming Alongside People Touched By Disability.* (P&R Publishing, 2006).

Joni Eareckson Tada, *Special Needs, Special Ministry.* (Group Publishing, 2003).

Special Needs Ministry Online Resources

The Christian Learning Center (CLC Network), www.clcnetwork.org

The Inclusive Church, https://theinclusivechurch.wordpress.com

The Irresistible Church,

Joni and Friends, http://www.joniandfriends.org

Key Ministry, http://www.keyministry.org

Special Needs and Disability Ministry Leaders Forum (Facebook group), https://www.facebook.com/groups/snadleaders/

Special Needs Parent Network, www.snappin.org

ACKNOWLEDGMENTS

Lord Jesus, You did all this. You've made us strong in once broken places. You took what the enemy intended for harm and converted them into blessings: a mysterious, spiritual alchemy only a loving and sovereign God could do. My apologies for all that kicking and screaming back there: You knew what You were doing after all. Not only that, You planted key saints along the way to breathe this book into reality.

Debbie Lillo, my Special Needs Ministry mentor. "You should write a book," you said. That was almost a decade ago. I can never thank you enough for how generously you've coached, counseled, and prayed me through many ministry "dangers, toils, and snares" since. I am where I am, and doing what I get to do, because of you. I relish how He brought us together, "for such a time as this," dear Mordi.

Amy Fenton Lee, you've modeled passion, pioneering, prophecy, and perseverance in breathtaking ways. I can't thank you enough for how you've encouraged, affirmed, and guided me in writing and especially through the prickly parts of ministry. Your friendship and generosity have blessed me in ways you'll never know. I'm indebted to you for letting me trail in your shadow.

Jessie Kirkland, my visionary agent, wise counsel, and praying friend. I barely had time to muse, "When I grow up, I'd want an agent just like her," when you plucked me from obscurity and launched me into publishing. Your confidence in me has been a priceless gift. Thank you for believing and drawing out the passions I scarcely believed He deposited in me.

Kathi Lipp, my Author Fairy Godmother. Serving on your team has been one of the timeliest blessings of my life. I didn't just gain an internship, but a role model in leadership, biz-smarts, people-smarts, generosity, and compassion. Most of all, I gained a cherished friend and mentor whom I love. Thank you for everything you've invested in me. It's an honor to stoke the "flames of holy discontent" with you.

Pamela Clements, Marilyn Jansen, Cat Hoort, and team at Worthy, it is not lost on me that you deemed a niche book for special-needs families "Worthy" of attention and investment. You had all my heart and hustle the moment you expressed willingness to serve this underserved audience, however small. You took a chance on us. I hope I've made you proud, and that God rewards your commitment to serve the least of the least of these. Your efforts have so reflected His heart!

Gisele, Christina, Delia, and Sarah, Joni Eareckson Tada has her beloved team of "Get Up Girls," who help her get up and out of the house every day. I have been richly blessed with you: my own squad of Get Up Girls, who help me do this overwhelming life. Thank you for your cheerleading and generous support for my family. None of this would be possible without you.

Justin, as a sibling to a brother with special needs, you've learned early on that life on a broken planet can be unfair. You've been shaped with great compassion, empathy, flexibility, and insight, because of your brother. Your dad and I so appreciate the light and joy you bring to our family. I pray that our journey as a special-needs family convinces you that God always redeems and repurposes pain. And that He is always good.

Jeremy, you've been the sharpest tool in heaven's drawer to break, melt, and remold me. I thought you were my project to help fix. I was wrong. God has used you immeasurably to humble, fix, and sanctify me. Thank you. We strive, believe, pray, advocate, and testify because of who and how God made you. When we all get to heaven and hear your resurrection voice, among many other long-awaited explanations, I hope you'll say, "It's okay, Mom. You did the best you could, given your own limitations. It's all good, now . . ."

Mr. and Mrs. Dokko, my devoted and ever-supportive parents. For every early-morning prayer meeting, for every dollar of private school tuition paid in hard-earned cash, for every frozen Ziploc of Korean food, for every American Dream that twisted into a heartache, for every untranslatable longing, for every desire and personal ambition you sacrificed to enable those of your children—and for so much more—a million thank-yous will never be enough. 사랑합니다.

Eddie, my loving and long-suffering husband. This book would never have seen its start or finish without your steadfast commitment, support, and sacrifice. The world may never know how much you give up for others. But God knows, and I'm a beneficiary of your servant-leadership every day. For nineteen years, you've kept the cap on my crazy and provided the safety and security our family enjoys. Every wife should have such a faithful and selfless husband; every child, such a loving and dedicated father; and every human, such a godly, loyal, and honorable friend.

And to the countless ministry leaders and volunteers who serve special-needs families. When we pick up our kids at the close of every respite event, you ask, "So, what did you do with your time off?"

This. I wrote this. It took forty-six years, every single respite, every Joni and Friends Family Retreat, and every Sunday worship service supported by a disability ministry to bring this book to fruition. Your sweaty (and probably stressed) sacrifice of running around after my kids for several hours, it matters. What you do makes a difference. Thank you.

Thank you all.

NOTES

Chapter 3

1. C. S. Lewis, *Mere Christianity* (New York: Touchstone, 1996), 176.

Chapter 5

2. Joni Eareckson Tada, *Anger: Aim It in the Right Direction* (Peabody: Rose Publishing, 2012).
3. Joni Eareckson Tada, *Anger: Aim It in the Right Direction*, quote by Dr. Dan Allender, (Peabody: Rose Publishing, 2012).
4. Henri J. M. Nouwen, introduction to *May I Hate God?* by Pierre Wolff (Mahwah: Paulist Press, 1979), 2.
5. Leonard Pine, "Remonstrating with God in Adversity: A Study in Habakkuk," *WRS Journal* 3:1 (February 1996): 21–26. http://wrs.edu/Materials_for_Web_Site/Journals/3-1%20Feb-1996/Pine%20-%20Remonstrating%20with%20God%20-%20Habakkuk.pdf.

Chapter 7

6. Elizabeth Eliot, *The Glad Surrender* (Ada: Revell, 2006).

Chapter 10

7. Joni Eareckson Tada, "God Permits What He Hates," Joni and Friends, May 15, 2013, http://www.joniandfriends.org/radio/4-minute/god-permits-what-he-hates1/.
8. Rick Warren's Facebook page, July 19, 2013, https://www.facebook.com/pastorrickwarren/posts/10151783860900903.

Chapter 12

9. Ken Blanchard and Phil Hodges, *Lead Like Jesus: Lessons for Everyone from the Greatest Leadership Role Model of All Time* (Nashville: Thomas Nelson, 2005), 199.
10. Henry Blackaby, Richard Blackaby, and Claude King, *Experiencing God: Knowing and Doing the Will of God* (Nashville: B&H Publishing Group, 2008), 121-122.
11. Ibid.
12. Henry T. Blackaby, *Created To Be God's Friend: How God Shapes Those He Loves* (Nashville: Thomas Nelson., 1999).
13. Blackaby, *Experiencing God.*

Chapter 15

14. Martin Luther King, Jr., April 16, 1963 "Letter from Birmingham City Jail," The King Center, The Archive, Atlanta.

Chapter 17

15. C. S. Lewis, *The Four Loves* (New York: HarperCollins, 1971).

Chapter 19

16. Joni Eareckson Tada, *A Lifetime of Wisdom: Embracing the Way God Heals You* (Grand Rapids: Zondervan, 2008), 28.

17. Joni Eareckson Tada, *A Place of Healing: Wrestling with the Mysteries of Suffering, Pain, and God's Sovereignty* (Colorado Springs: David C Cook, 2010), 49.
18. Ibid., 56.

Chapter 20

19. Jim Elliot. *The Journals of Jim Elliot*; https://www.goodreads.com/quotes/386936-god-always-gives-his-best-to-those-who-leave-the.
20. Joni Eareckson Tada, *Joni: An Unforgettable Story* (Grand Rapids: Zondervan, 2001).

Chapter 21

21. Wayne Barber, Eddie Rasnake, and Richard Shepherd, *Life Principles from the New Testament Men of Faith* (Chattanooga: A M G Publishers, 1999), 106-107.

Chapter 25

22. Joni Eareckson Tada, *A Place of Healing: Wrestling with the Mysteries of Suffering, Pain, and God's Sovereignty* (Colorado Springs: David C Cook, 2010), 56.

Chapter 27

23. *Public Papers of the Presidents of the United States: George W. Bush, 2004*, Book II (Washington, D.C.: Government Publishing Office), 1855-1863.

Chapter 28

24. Anonymous, Bible Study Tools; https://www.biblestudytools.com/pastor-resources/illustrations/to-illustrate-christ-11645866.html

Chapter 29

25. Jack Wellman, "Oswald Chambers: Biography, Quotes and Role in Christian History," *Christian Crier* (blog), Patheos, May 25, 2014, http://www.patheos.com/blogs/christiancrier/2014/05/25/oswald-chambers-biography-quotes-and-role-in-christian-history/.

ABOUT THE AUTHOR

Diane's passion is to encourage struggling parents with the timeless relevance of Scripture as applied to the gritty realities of special-needs family life. Challenges are a unique opportunity for discipleship, spiritual growth, and transformation. In 2004, her first son was diagnosed with autism at age two and ADHD, which triggered profound personal, professional, and spiritual crises.

In 2008, with comfort received from Christ (2 Corinthians 1:4), she began serving the disabled community as a special-needs ministry consultant. She equips churches to be inclusive faith communities, leads parent support groups, and speaks at churches and conferences. Diane partners with the ministries of *Joni and Friends* as a national speaker and ministry ambassador. In 2012, she launched an online ministry. Her writing has been featured in Orange's *Parent Cue, Parenting Magazine, Dandelion Magazine,* and SpecialNeedsParenting.net.

Diane and her husband, Eddie, have served over twenty-five years in bi-vocational ministry. They live in the heart of Silicon Valley with their two young sons.

Connect with her at www.dianedokkokim.com, where she blogs on being wrecked, redeemed, and repurposed.

IF YOU ENJOYED THIS BOOK, WILL YOU CONSIDER SHARING THE MESSAGE WITH OTHERS?

Mention the book in a blog post or through Facebook, Twitter, Pinterest, or upload a picture through Instagram.

Recommend this book to those in your small group, book club, workplace, and classes.

Head over to facebook.com/worthypublishing, "LIKE" the page, and post a comment as to what you enjoyed the most.

Tweet "I recommend reading #UnbrokenFaith by @Diane Dokko Kim // @worthypub"

Pick up a copy for someone you know who would be challenged and encouraged by this message.

Write a book review online.

Visit us at worthypublishing.com

twitter.com/worthypub

instagram.com/worthypub

facebook.com/worthypublishing

youtube.com/worthypublishing